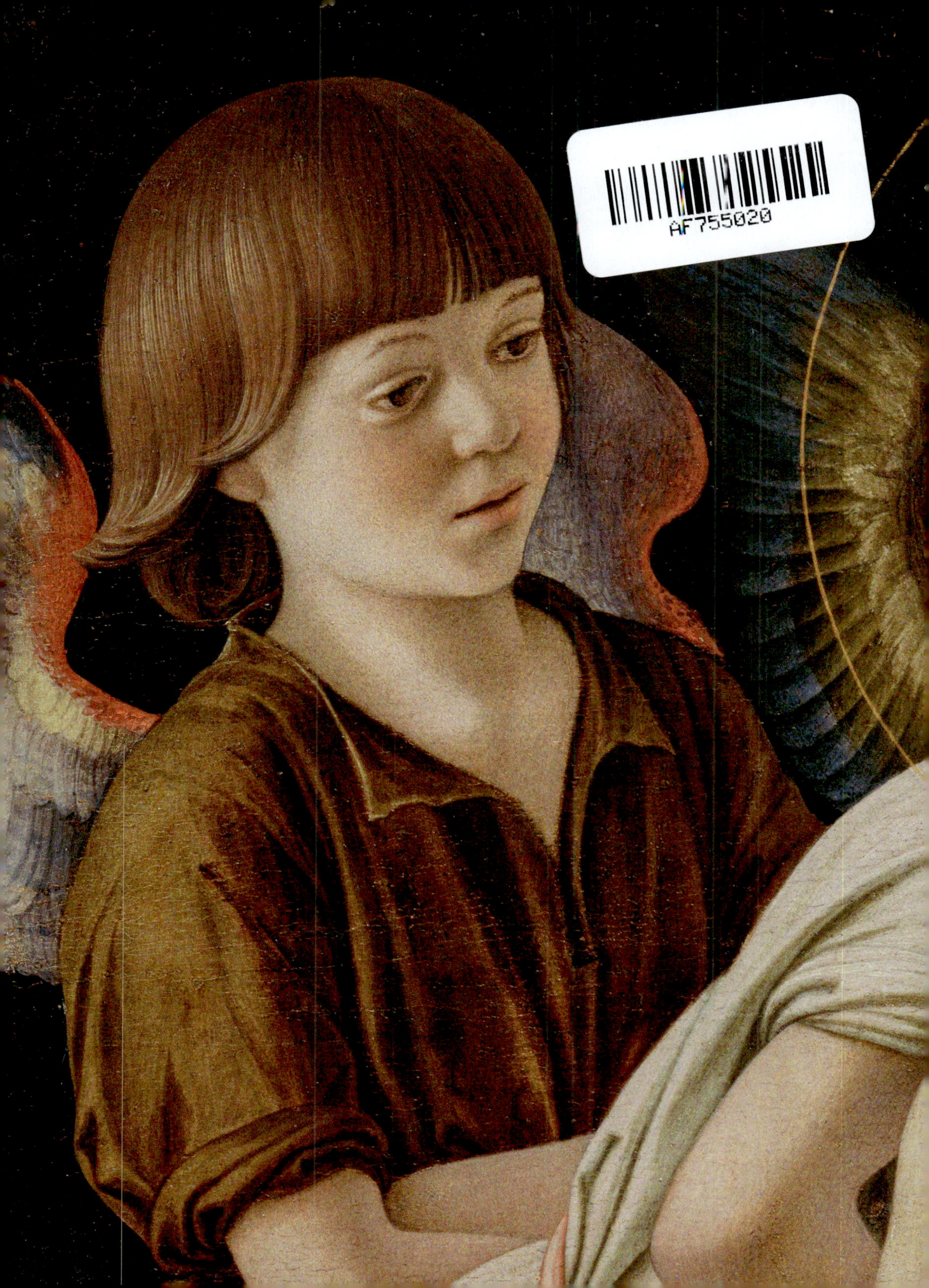

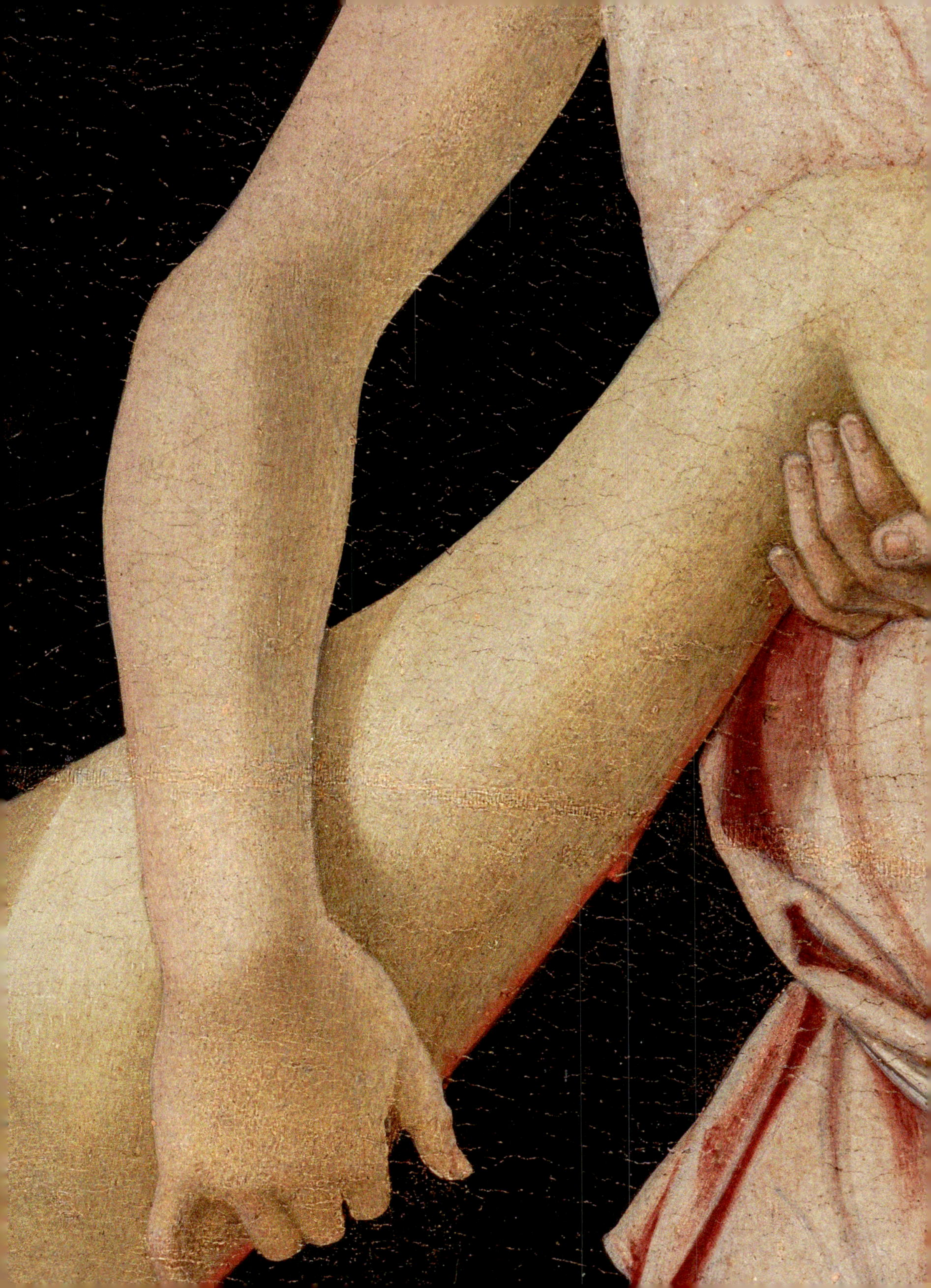

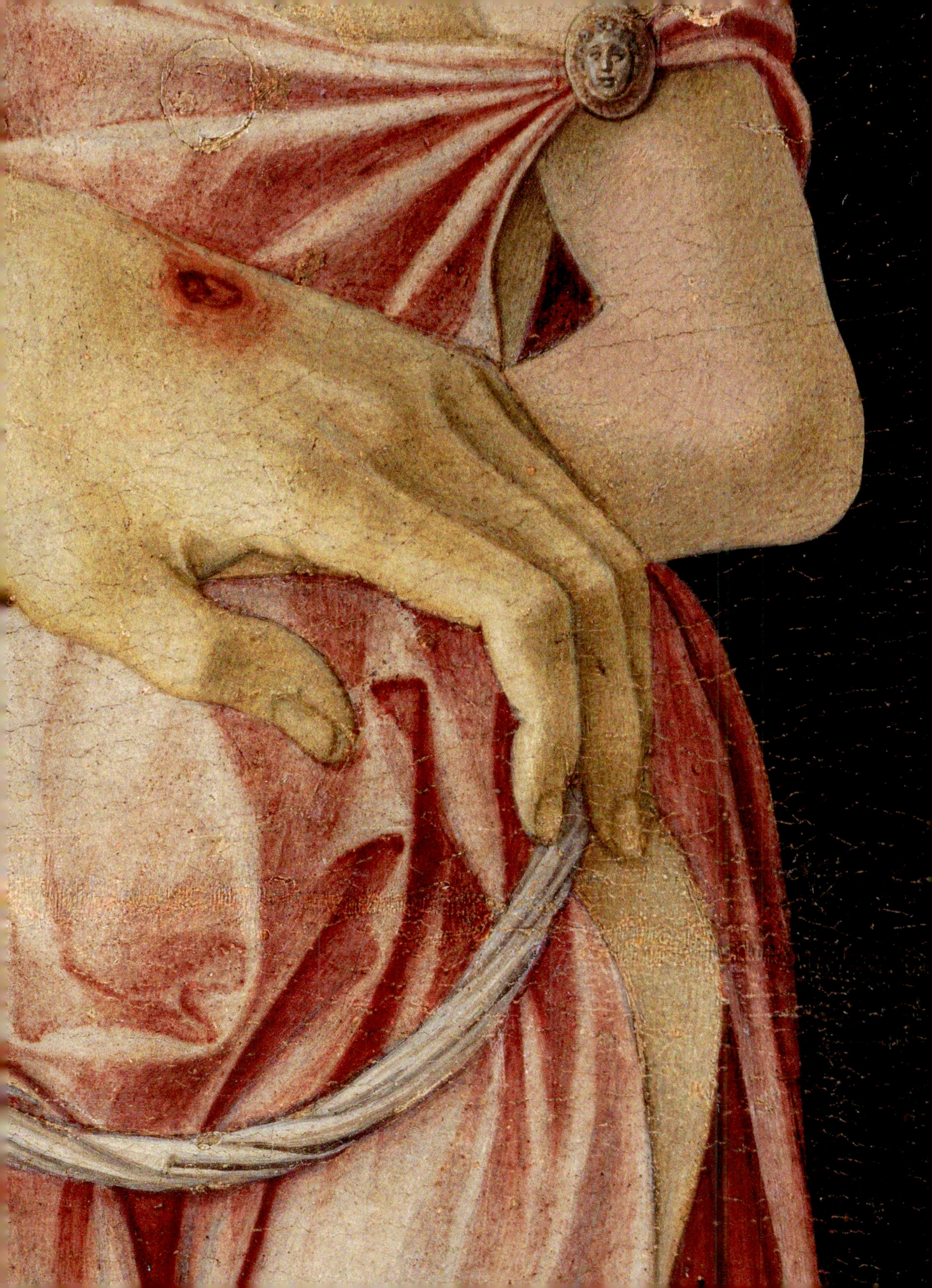

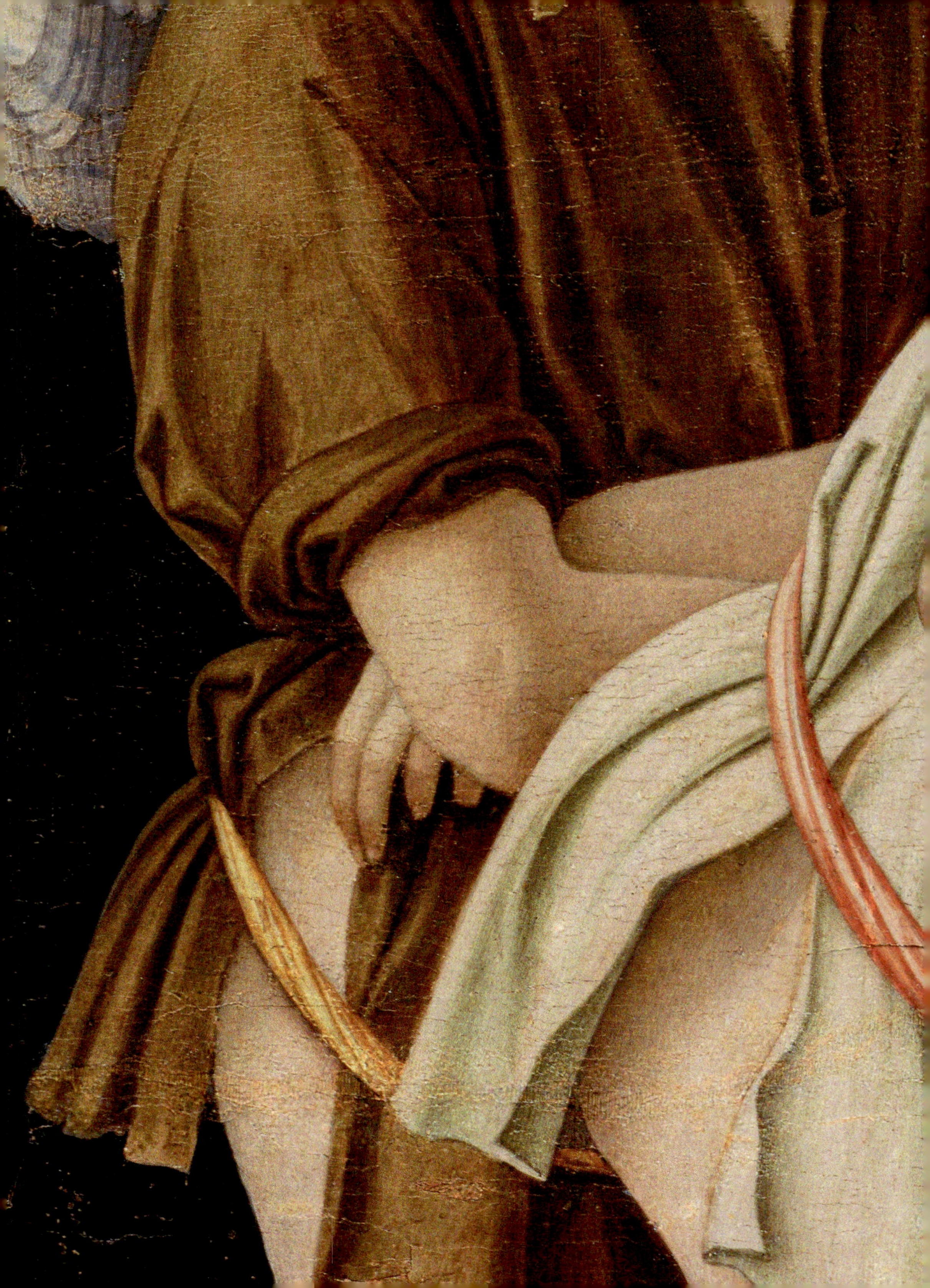

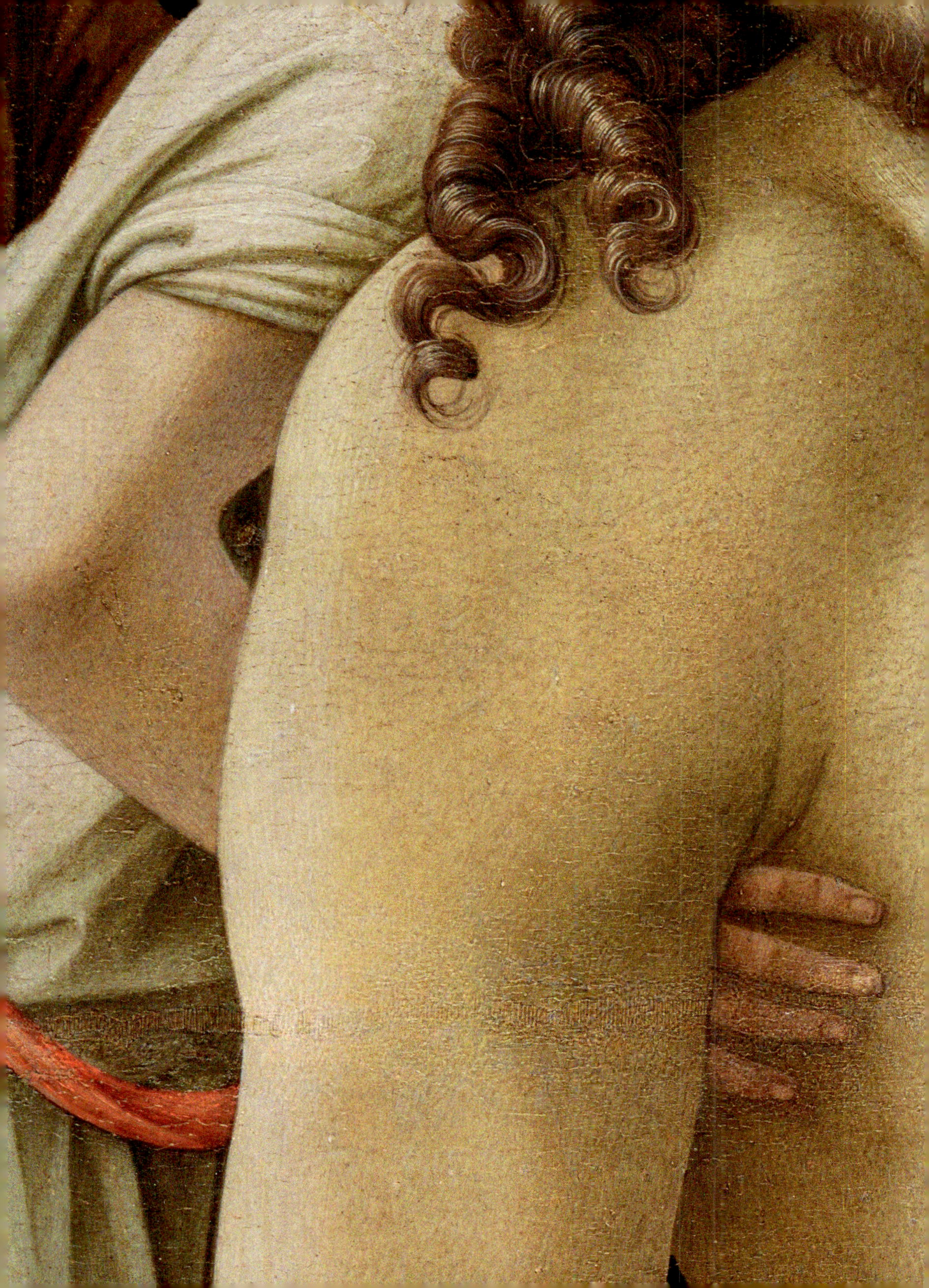

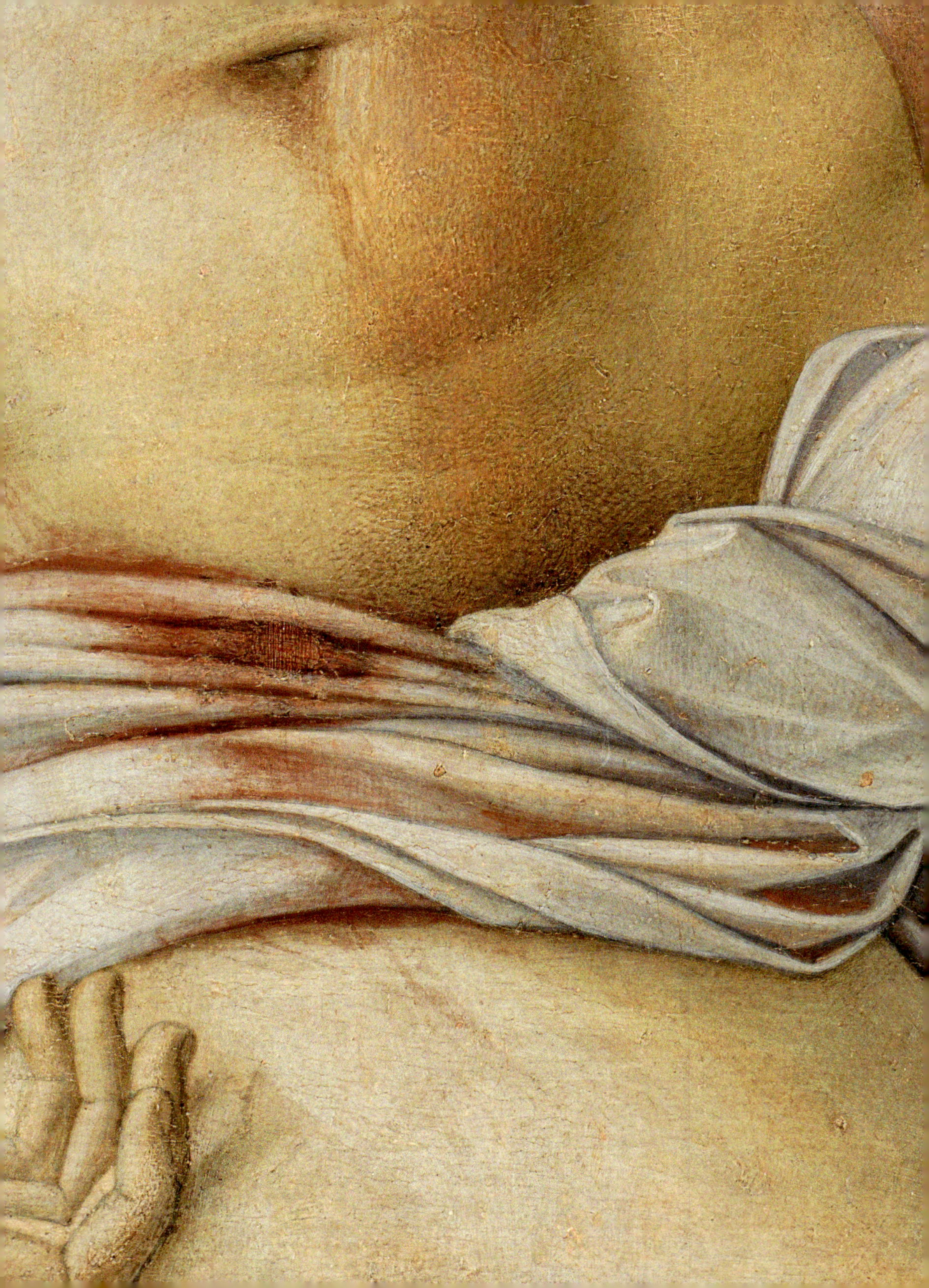

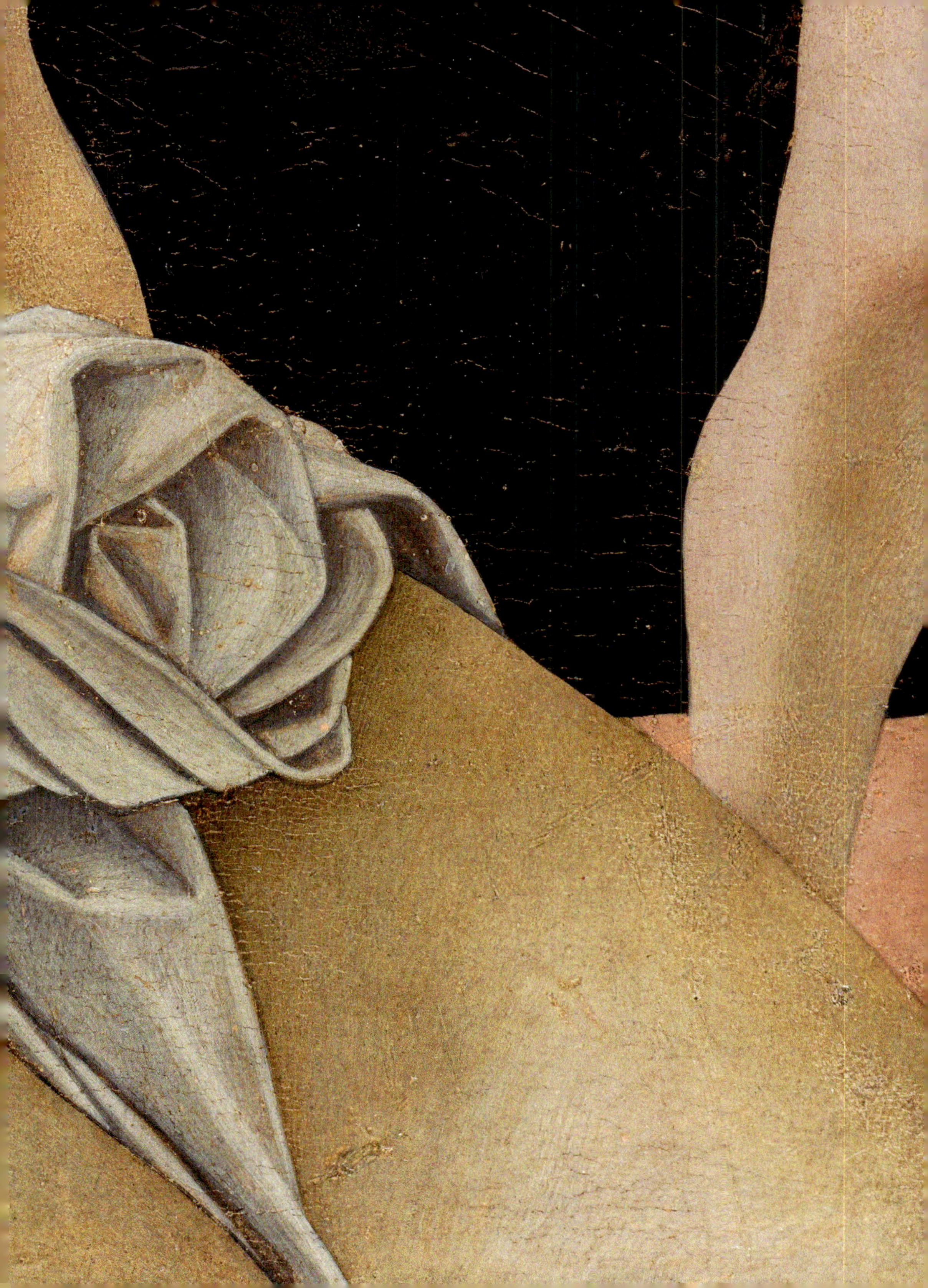

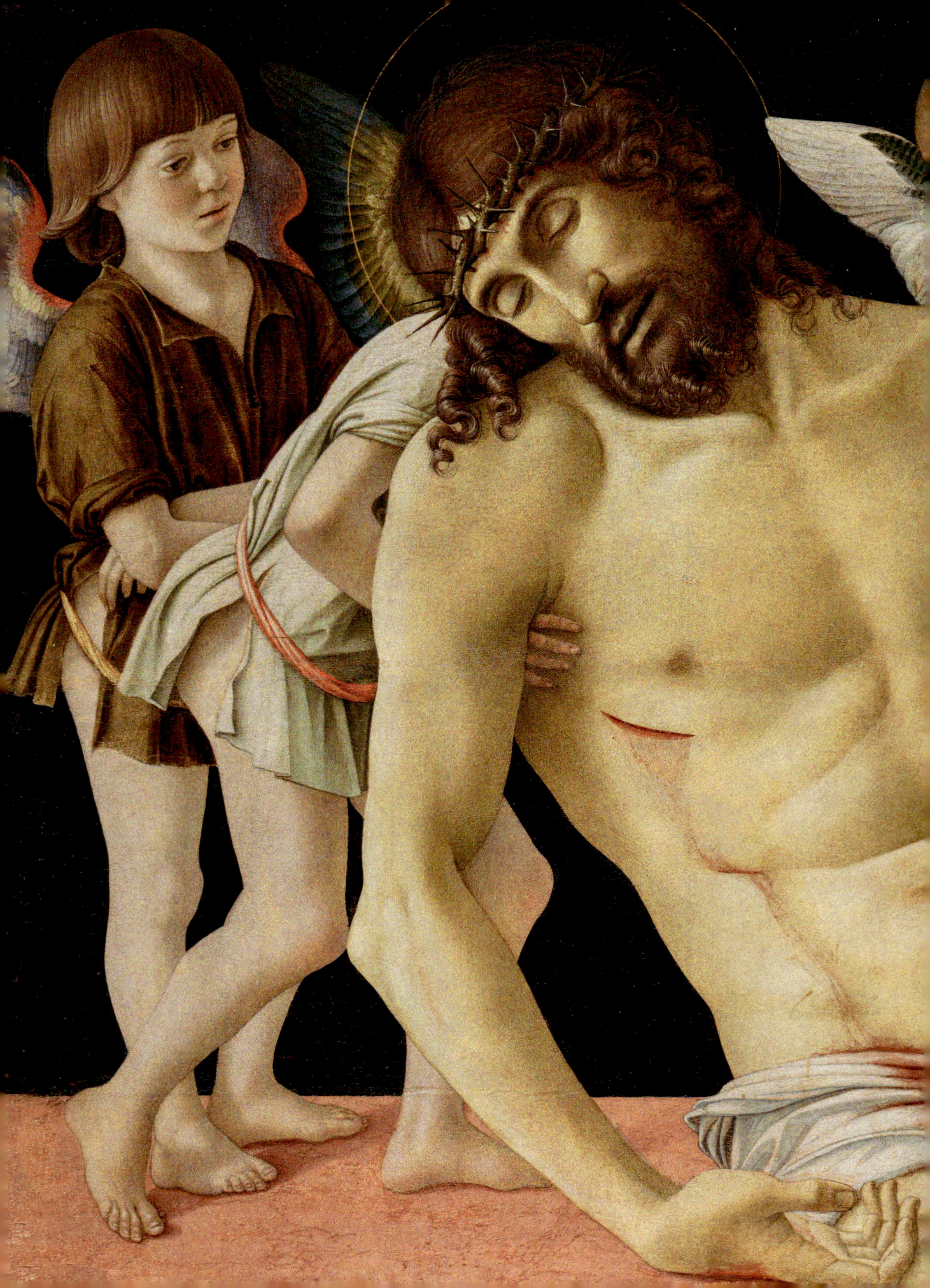

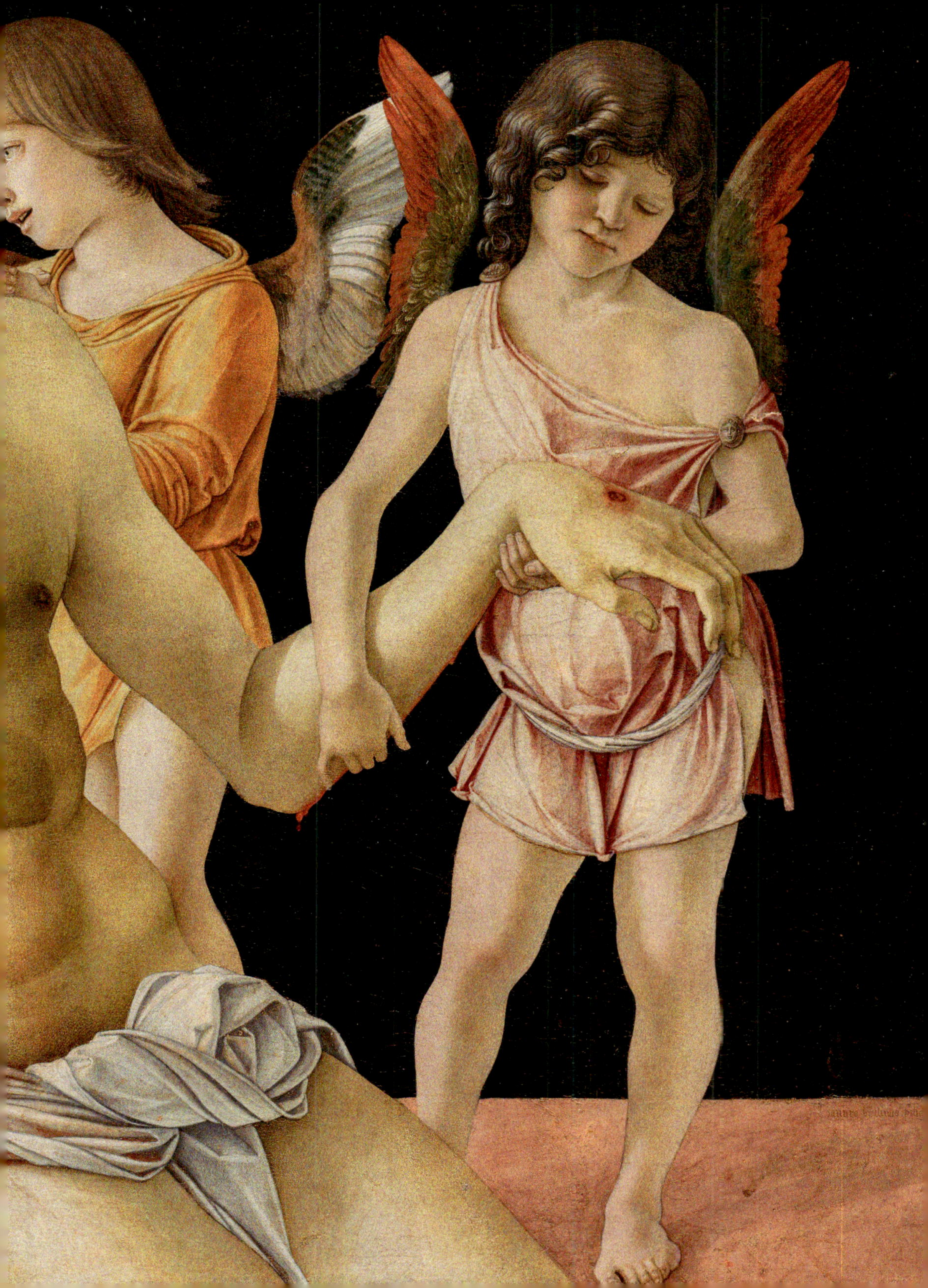

The publication of this volume has been financed by

VENETIAN
HERITAGE

Giovanni Bellini's Pietà

restored by

Venetian Heritage

Marsilio Arte

Giovanni Bellini's Pietà

restored by
Venetian Heritage

Venice,
Galleria Giorgio Franchetti
alla Ca' d'Oro
November 21, 2025
—January 6, 2026

New York,
The Morgan Library & Museum
January 15
—April 19, 2026

Promoted by

VENETIAN HERITAGE

MINISTERO DELLA CULTURA

DIREZIONE REGIONALE MUSEI NAZIONALI VENETO

GALLERIA GIORGIO FRANCHETTI ALLA CA'D'ORO

MUSEI ITALIANI

Comune di Rimini

rimini musei

The Morgan Library & Museum

Financed by
Venetian Heritage

Exhibition curated by
Toto Bergamo Rossi
Giovanni Sassu

Organization of the exhibition
Toto Bergamo Rossi
Alessandra Cecchetto
Valentina Farace

Administrative organization
for Venetian Heritage
Giorgio Ceccato
for the Municipality of Rimini
Serena Amati
Alessandro Giovanardi
Francesca Minak
Silvia Moni

Lenders
Comune di Rimini - Museo
della Città "Luigi Tonini"

Diagnostic analysis
STArt-Test di S. Schiavone & C. sas

Restoration
CBC – Conservazione Beni Culturali

Alta sorveglianza / Scientific
Supervision for the Soprintendenza
Archeologia Belle Arti e Paesaggio
per le province di Ravenna, Forlì-
Cesena e Rimini
Luca Giorgini
in collaboration with
Sonia Revelant

Restoration funded by
François Droulers, Fondazione
Venetian Heritage, Venice
Marco Voena, Venetian Heritage
Inc., New York

Transport
Arterìa

Insurance
ARTE Generali

Exhibition set-up
UNISVE

Lighting design
Studio Pasetti

Lighting
Spazioluce

Graphic design
Livio Cassese

Printing of graphics
in the exhibition
Gruppofallani

Educational materials
Toto Bergamo Rossi
Alessandra Cecchetto
Giovanni Sassu

Press office
Giovanni Maria Sgrignuoli
with
Matilde Buzzoni
Federica Marra

Catalog texts
Maria Francesca Alberghina
Toto Bergamo Rossi
Peter Humfrey
Sara Masinelli
Giovanni Sassu
Salvatore Schiavone
Lucia Tito
Giulio Zavatta

Photographs
Matteo De Fina

Translations
Gabriele Poole

Acknowledgements
Elizabeth Abbarno
Maria Francesca Alberghina
Serena Amati
Colin B. Bailey
Roberto Barison
Caterina Barnaba
Elena Buriola
Alvise di Canossa
Italo Carli
Alex Félix
Luca Giorgini
Alessandro Giovanardi
Federica Gonzato
Christine Hearst Schwarzman
Guido Jaccarino
Katia Jancikic
Michele Lari
Carlo Alberto Manzan
John Marciari
Martina Mian
Francesca Minak
Silvia Moni
Elisabetta Pasca
Alberto Pasetti Bombardella
Giulia Passante
Alessandro Pedron
Marco Pradelli
Sonia Revelant
Kate Robinson
Jamil Sadegholvaad
Salvatore Schiavone
Silvia Scocco
Lucia Tito
Gilberto Urbinati

MINISTERO DELLA CULTURA

Minister
Alessandro Giuli

Secretary General
Mario Turetta

Director General of Museums
Massimo Osanna

DIREZIONE REGIONALE MUSEI NAZIONALI VENETO

Director
Daniele Ferrara

Secretary
Lorena Muran

Contracts Office
Francesco Maraldo

Exhibitions Department
Maria Francesca De Pasquali

Technical Office
Annunziata Genchi
Chiara Matteazzi
Giulia Passante
Elena Riu
Mauro Tarantino
Francesco Tinè

Archives
Marta Boscolo Marchi

Photographic archives
Anna Granzotto

Promotion, communication, Press Office, and Web Site
Maria Teresa Dal Bò
Elisabetta Pasqualin

Educational
Elisabetta Pasqualin

Health & safety manager
Ettore Bogoni (Società Consilia)

GALLERIA GIORGIO FRANCHETTI ALLA CA' D'ORO

Director
Claudia Cremonini

Art Historian
Paola Bressan

Conservators
Barbara Biciocchi
Daniele Pasta
Sonia Revelant

Access security and reception assistants of the Galleria Giorgio Franchetti alla Ca' d'Oro
Gloria De Faveri, Eber Fraccaro, Barbara Marangoni, Enzo Marzi, Moreno Osselladore, Maria Pertosa, Fabrizia Rizzuto, Mario Rosso, Loredana Spinnato, Sabrina Tenan, Marco Toso, Antonella Tranquillini
in collaboration with
Verona 83 - Soc. Coop A.R.L.

The publication of the volume was financed by Fondazione Venetian Heritage, Venice, thanks to the donation of Board Member Roger Thomas and with the support of the Board of Directors of Venetian Heritage Inc., New York

Jamil Sadegholvaad

Mayor, City of Rimini

It should be like when children leave home: we say goodbye with a mix of sadness and happiness. We wish them a safe journey, trust that their new experiences will help them grow, and look forward to the exchange that follows—what they learn, they bring back and share.

It should be the same, now that this masterpiece of art history, a favorite child of Rimini, this unique provincial town in Italy, is leaving us for Venice. We know it will return in a few months. And we know it will be changed, with nuances that will be new to all those who have admired it in recent decades, closer to the original idea of its famous creator and yet (or precisely for this reason) better able to engage with the contemporary world.

This is the spirit with which the City of Rimini approaches this cultural project, in synergy with Fondazione Venetian Heritage. A project that marks the beginning of a new, more conscious season in the relationship between Rimini and its art and culture. A sort of age of reason, if you will, in which our greatest investment (economic, social, and collective) is made in "durable goods." And yet, we understand "durable" in the most dynamic sense: a work of art rediscovered and restored to its former brilliance, thanks to the care of experts and the wonders of technology, not only renews our desire to engage with it but also sparks curiosity, anticipation, and passion for the future of our community.

Few cities in the world know how to be modern in their contradictions like Rimini. It is precisely this constant balance—between Bellini's *Pietà* (*Dead Christ supported by Four Angels*), Leon Battista Alberti's Temple, the Roman remains, and, at the same time, the city's identity as a beloved (sometimes too beloved) holiday destination—that makes this "dot on the Adriatic" unique. And so, as with the child who leaves only to return a different person, we await this masterpiece's homecoming, ready for it to continue nourishing the art, history, and myth of Rimini.

Alessandro Giovanardi

Director, Musei Comunali di Rimini

Perhaps no painting better embodies, through the silent music of its gestures, the spirit of the Renaissance in Rimini than Giovanni Bellini's *Pietà* (*Dead Christ supported by Four Angels*).

Despite the diversity of disciplines and styles, the Venetian master's work immediately calls to mind the Tempio Malatestiano; the architectural and philosophical thought of Leon Battista Alberti; the medals of Pisanello and Matteo de' Pasti; the dramatic serenity of Piero della Francesca; and the cherubs and celestial messengers of Agostino di Duccio.

With its exquisitely refined harmony of colors—now rediscovered through its recent restoration—the panel has long been regarded as the most precious treasure of the city's museum collections. It is undoubtedly the most requested painting, and the one that has traveled most widely in Italy and abroad, as it is considered a key link in the industrious workshop that was fifteenth-century painting in general, and in particular, in Bellini's oeuvre.

The work stands almost as an emblem between the Po Valley culture of the Renaissance courts—connected to the tense and dramatic classicism of Andrea Mantegna (who in 1453 married Nicolosia, Giovanni Bellini's sister)—and a necessary rootedness in Adriatic and Mediterranean culture. On one hand lies the tragic humanism so finely analyzed by Massimo Cacciari; on the other, the mysterious Hellenizing idealism that suspends Christ and the winged youths in an atmosphere of fabula mystica.

It is no coincidence that Roger Fry evoked the ancient Greek red-figure vase painting against a dark ground, while Hans Belting emphasized the work's nature as a true sacred icon—a quality that Bellini sought to preserve, even as he reinterpreted it in a new light.

It would be a mistake, therefore, not to recognize the liturgical and Eucharistic spirit that permeates every detail, every gesture, every movement of the painting. The restrained tears of the *Pietà*, as it is commonly known, form a genuine Greek *threnos* transplanted into the humanistic rebirth—ascending, through Bellini "first Gothic and Byzantine, then Mantegnesque and Paduan, then following in the footsteps of Piero and Antonello" (Roberto Longhi)—back to the timeless sources of the ritual of lamentation, a symbolic font of purification and wisdom.

Daniele Ferrara
Director, Direzione regionale Musei nazionali Veneto

Claudia Cremonini
Director, Galleria Giorgio Franchetti alla Ca' d'Oro

The restoration of Giovanni Bellini's *Pietà* (*Dead Christ supported by Four Angels*), carried out at the Galleria Giorgio Franchetti alla Ca' d'Oro, is significant for several reasons.
First and foremost, it represents the successful outcome of a collaboration between the public and private sectors, specifically the Italian Ministry, the City of Rimini and the Fondazione Venetian Heritage. We are deeply grateful for the foundation's support and its far-reaching vision of our cultural heritage, consistent with the extensive national and international dissemination of the cultural heritage of the ancient Republic of Venice and the many institutions that are consequently responsible for its protection.
Secondly, the ambitious and complex restoration project was carried out within the adjoining palaces of Ca' d'Oro and Palazzo Duodo—an arrangement that itself recalls the historic partnership between the Superintendency, then directed by Gino Fogolari, and Baron Giorgio Franchetti.
On this occasion, the restoration laboratory—originally established in the aftermath of the 1966 flood to repair damage to sculptures and paintings – has been reactivated, and is now once again available thanks to the presence of restorers and art historians, ready to collaborate with museums and other local institutions. The reactivation of the laboratory is part of a more general reorganization of the entire museum carried out by Venetian Heritage, along with the technicians, custodians, and the

administration staff of the Direzione regionale Musei nazionali Veneto, as well as professionals and specialized firms.

The restoration, carried out by Lucia Tito, also forms part of a broader study aimed at investigating the original significance of the painting, considering it as evidence of private interests, linked to the specific commission, but also of public ones, insofar as the painting bears witness to the links between the Republic of Venice and the Malatesta family of Rimini. In this sense, the initiative is part of a joint project between the Direzione regionale and the Municipality of Rimini, which will also include an exhibition featuring the *Pietà* alongside Mantegna's *San Sebastiano*. The works of the two masters will be used to reconstruct the context of cultural exchanges and artistic influences that took place between Venice, Rimini, and the Po Valley in the second half of the fifteenth century, helping develop the relations between the various centers and, in particular, between Venice and Rimini, two cities facing the Adriatic, in the context of the political developments in which they were involved.

While the connection between Alberti and Mantegna is well known, the project will also call attention to the lesser-known role played by Leon Battista Alberti in designing the Tempio Malatestiano following the commission by Sigismondo Malatesta, a project which, also through the works of Mauro Codussi, was a crucial step in the development of Venetian and Adriatic Renaissance architecture.

In addition to the *Pietà* commissioned by a patron in Rimini, other works by Bellini bear witness to the painter's close relation with the Romagna region: the altarpiece made for Pesaro, the citation of monuments in Rimini and Ravenna in his landscapes. This aspect of Bellini's work will be examined in the context of the influence in Romagna of the style and themes of Mantegna (Giovanni Francesco da Rimini, Ansuino da Forlì, Bono da Ferrara, etc.) and of Bellini (Lattanzio da Rimini, Benedetto Coda, Marco Palmezzano, Niccolò Rondinelli, etc.). Aspects that, in turn, must be understood in the context of the relationship with Venice cultivated by humanists from Romagna, such as Pietro Parleone from Rimini and Lidio Catti from Ravenna. These are ideas and stimuli to be developed in future initiatives, envisioned within a polycentric and multicultural Adriatic context.

Federica Gonzato

Superintendent, Soprintendenza Archeologia, Belle Arti e Paesaggio
per le province di Ravenna, Forlì-Cesena e Rimini

The present volume celebrates the happy result of Fondazione Venetian Heritage's generous financial support of the restoration and exhibition of a fundamental work, Giovanni Bellini's *Pietà* (*Dead Christ supported by Four Angels*), and of the collaboration between all the Institutions that have worked tirelessly to ensure the success of the initiative. Although obvious, it is worth underlining once more the outstanding importance of Bellini's *Pietà*, certainly the most representative work of the Museo della Città di Rimini "Luigi Tonini". An iconic work par excellence, as confirmed by the fact that we see (and *want* to see) its reproduction on museum banners, posters, brochures, and promotional material. The initiative we celebrate today is also meant to give the city's most important work of art the visibility it deserves. But allow me the pleasure to say a few words about this masterpiece.

The painting was kept for centuries in the famous Tempio Malatestiano. It was only in the first half of the nineteenth century that it was moved to the town hall first and then to the Pinacoteca di Rimini. The painting is dated to the 1470s. Giorgio Vasari in his *Vite*, does write that Bellini, "painted a large Pietà in Arimino [Rimini] for Signor Sigismondo Malatesti, with two cherubs supporting it, which is now in S. Francesco in that city...". This would date it necessarily to before the death of Sigismondo, in 1468, but based on stylistic analysis and comparison with other works by Bellini, most scholars reject this dating.

In 1962, Augusto Campana published the will of Rainerio di Ludovico Migliorati, advisor to Pandolfo IV Malatesta, dated February 17, 1499, along with the attached inventory. In the will, Migliorati mentions the *Pietà*, assigning it to a chapel where his remains were to be housed in the church of Sant'Antonio, adjacent the church of San Francesco. The document is clear evidence of how the work was "inseparable" from Rimini from the beginning. It was and remains, I repeat, an essential and outstanding element of the identity of the museum, of the town, and of its territory.

Another happy coincidence that I would like to mention is the timing of the restoration: the first agreements between the parties on the restoration took shape in 2024, exactly 100 years after the inauguration of the first Pinacoteca of Rimini. A new beginning, for the work and for the museum that houses it.

The painting was first restored in 1929 by Mauro Pellicioli, prior to its transfer to London for the famous exhibition on Italian painting. On that occasion, the Podestà of Rimini authorized the replacement of the fixed cradling with a movable system. In 1949, Pellicioli worked on the painting again, correcting a chromatic alteration before another exhibition to be held at the Doge's Palace in Venice. In 1969, the restoration was undertaken by Ottorino Nonfarmale and Otello Caprara, who were forced to remove the entire wooden panel, severely damaged by woodworm that had thrived unnoticed beneath the Florentine-style parquet backing. This intervention remains the most significant restoration carried out on the work. A final intervention dates back to 2019, when, upon opening the museum crate used to transport the painting from an exhibition in London to one in Berlin, it was discovered that the packaging material had attached itself to the paint surface in several places. The damage was repaired by Adele Pompili. During the present restoration carried out by Lucia Tito, a thick layer of uneven yellowing varnish was removed. The underlying paint film proved to be still perfectly bonded to the honeycomb aluminum support used by Nonfarmale in 1969. It was then decided how to intervene on the abrasions and the long crack in the center.

The collaboration of the Photographic Archive of the Pinacoteca di Bologna (formerly part of the Soprintendenza per i Beni Artistici e Storici per le Province di Bologna, Ferrara, Forlì–Cesena, Ravenna e Rimini) was invaluable. The photos of the back of the original panel before it was removed in 1969, found by my colleague Luca Giorgini, allow us to identify with greater precision the marks left by the panel on the paint film around the crack in the center. The recently completed restoration draws also on the rich documentation produced by the diagnostic studies authorized by the Superintendency of Ravenna, an essential preliminary phase.

Finally, I need to mention the relationship between Venice and Romagna, a region connecting central and northern Italy, often subject to Venetian rule, as in the case of Ravenna in particular. It is therefore not surprising that in this beautiful town we find numerous monuments and works of art that speak the language of the Republic of Venice and bear witness to the wide-spread presence of Venetian culture. Our final hope is that other works in need of restoration, located in the territory under the jurisdiction of the Superintendency of Ravenna, might benefit in the future from the attention of Venetian Heritage.

Valentina Marini Clarelli Nasi
President, Fondazione Venetian Heritage, Venice

Peter Marino
Chairman and President, Venetian Heritage Inc., New York

Since 1999, Venetian Heritage has been promoting Venetian culture through a vast campaign of restoration projects in Venice as well as in the territories that were once part of the Venetian Republic. This extensive and ambitious program has involved institutions, foundations, and private patrons, in Italy and abroad, all sharing the common goal of preserving the immense artistic heritage that the Republic of Venice disseminated throughout the eastern Mediterranean from the Middle Ages to the end of the eighteenth century. Venetian Heritage continues its active commitment to raising funds for the conservation and protection of this unique cultural heritage.

We are particularly proud to introduce the present catalog, which celebrates the restoration of a masterpiece of Venetian art: Giovanni Bellini's *Pietà* (*Dead Christ supported by Four Angels*).

We would like to express our most sincere gratitude to all those who made possible the restoration and exhibition at the Ca' d'Oro of this extraordinary painting. Our heartfelt thanks go first and foremost to the City of Rimini, and in particular to its Mayor, Jamil Sadegholvaad; to Michele Lari, Assessore alla Cultura; to Silvia Moni, Dirigente del Settore Sistemi Culturali di Città; to Serena Amati and Francesca Minak; and to Giovanni Sassu, former Director of the Musei di Rimini and co-curator of this special exhibition. Within the Soprintendenza Archeologia, Belle Arti e Paesaggio delle province di Ravenna, Forlì-Cesena e Rimini, our special thanks go to the Superintendent, Federica Gonzato, and the Art Historian, Luca Giorgini. Heartfelt thanks also go to the Direzione regionale Musei nazionali Veneto of the Italian Ministry of Culture, and in particular to its Director, Daniele Ferrara; to the Director of the Galleria Giorgio Franchetti alla Ca' d'Oro, Claudia Cremonini; and to the Conservator-Restorer, Sonia Revelant.

Special thanks go to CBC – Conservazione Beni Culturali and to conservator Lucia Tito, who restored the painting, to STArt-Test di S. Schiavone & C. sas for the diagnostic analyses, to Matteo De Fina for the photographic campaign, to Livio Cassese for the graphic design, to Gruppofallani for the graphic production, UNISVE for the exhibition set up, Spazioluce for the lighting installation, Studio Pasetti for the lighting design, Arterìa for transport and handling, and ARTE Generali for insurance.

Sincere thanks go to François Droulers, Board Member of Fondazione Venetian Heritage, Venice, and Marco Voena, Board Member of Venetian Heritage Inc., New York, for their generous support of the restoration work.

The publication of this volume was made possible thanks to a donation from Roger Thomas, Board Member of Fondazione Venetian Heritage, Venice, and with the support of the Board of Directors of Venetian Heritage Inc., New York. We would also like to thank the authors of this volume, Peter Humfrey, Sara Masinelli, Giovanni Sassu, and Giulio Zavatta, for their studies, which offer an updated and detailed discussion of Giovanni Bellini's *Pietà*, and all those who contributed to the creation of the catalog: Livio Cassese, Matteo De Fina, Martina Mian, Elisabetta Pasca, and Gabriele Poole.

Special thanks go to the staff of The Morgan Library & Museum in New York—Colin B. Bailey, Katharine J. Rayner Director; John Marciari, Director of Curatorial Affairs; Elizabeth Abbarno, Director of Exhibition and Collection Management; Kate Robinson, Exhibitions Registrar; and Alex Félix, Exhibition Coordinator—for enthusiastically embracing the exhibition project for Bellini's *Pietà*.

Very special thanks are also due to our team for their dedication and commitment to managing Venetian Heritage's activities: Giorgio Ceccato, Valentina Farace, Alessandra Cecchetto, and Elena Buriola from the Venice office, and Kory Trolio from the New York office. Finally, we would like to thank Toto Bergamo Rossi for organizing the restoration project for Giovanni Bellini's *Pietà* as well as its exhibition in Venice and New York.

Colin B. Bailey

Katharine J. Rayner Director, The Morgan Library & Museum

It is a great pleasure to exhibit Giovanni Bellini's *Pietà* (*Dead Christ supported by Four Angels*) from about 1470 at the Morgan Library & Museum. This masterpiece of the Venetian Renaissance shows Bellini at the height of his creative powers, embracing a long tradition of icon painting but instilling it with new life through his incorporation of Renaissance classicism and humanism, adding not only layers of meaning but also powerful emotion to the scene. Shown in the West Room of our historic library—Pierpont Morgan's private study—Bellini's *Pietà* will appear alongside other treasures of Italian Renaissance art by Bellini's contemporaries: sculpture by Antonio Rossellino and paintings by Perugino, Francesco Francia, Cima da Conegliano, as well as paintings by Hans Memling, who so influenced Italian Art in the last decades of the fifteenth century.

Our exhibition is made possible through a partnership with Venetian Heritage Inc., New York, which is responsible for the recent conservation of Bellini's painting and for this catalog. Our great thanks go above all to Peter Marino, the generous President of that organization, and to Toto Bergamo Rossi, the Director, who has worked closely at every stage of the project with the Morgan's John Marciari, Director of Curatorial Affairs, and Elizabeth Abbarno, Director of Exhibition and Collection Management.

We also thank Jamil Sadegholvaad, the Mayor of Rimini; Michele Lari, Assessore alla Cultura in Rimini; and Federica Gonzato, Superintendent,

Soprintendenza Archeologia, Belle Arti e Paesaggio per le province di Ravenna, Forlì-Cesena e Rimini, for agreeing to part with Bellini's painting for a few months so that it could be shown here in New York and make a visit to America for the very first time.

Photo credits
All the photographs published in this volume are by Matteo De Fina, courtesy of Rimini, Museo della Città "Luigi Tonini", except:

Archivio Nonfarmale di San Lazzaro di Savena, Bologna p. 92

© Barber Institute of Fine Arts / © The Henry Barber Trust, The Barber Institute of Fine Arts, University of Birmingham / Bridgeman Images p. 54

Biblioteca civica Gambalunga, Archivio fotografico pp. 81, 82, 85 fig. 9, 86

Biblioteca civica Gambalunga, Archivio fotografico / photo Minghini p. 89

2025 © Biblioteca Correr - Fondazione Musei Civici di Venezia p. 79

Cameraphoto Arte p. 42

CISA Andrea Palladio, Vicenza p. 66

Courtesy of Ministero della Cultura – Archivio Fotografico dei Musei Nazionali di Bologna - Direzione regionale Musei Nazionali Emilia-Romagna pp. 101, 103

Courtesy of Fondazione Musei Civici di Venezia pp. 44-45, 48

Photo Gilberto Urbinati p. 69

© Illustrated London News Ltd. / Mary Evans p. 85 fig. 8

Museo della Città "Luigi Tonini", Rimini / photo Gilberto Urbinati p. 78

Nationalmuseum, Public domain p. 46 fig. 5

Photo Scala, Florence pp. 43, 46 fig. 4, 50

© Pinacoteca di Brera, Milano – MiC p. 47

© 2008 Scuderie del Quirinale, "Giovanni Bellini" December 19, 2008 – May 10, 2009 / photo Alfredo Cacciani p. 93

© The National Gallery, London / Scala, Firenze p. 49

© Victoria and Albert Museum, London p. 51

Every reasonable attempt has been made to identify the copyright owners. Errors or omissions reported to the publisher will be corrected in subsequent editions.

Cover
Giovanni Bellini,
Pietà, circa 1470, detail
Rimini, Museo della Città
"Luigi Tonini"

Translation
Gabriele Poole

Design and layout
Livio Cassese

Typesetting
Rosanna Alberti

First Edition November 2025

ISBN 979-12-5463-344-1
www.marsilioeditori.it

Printed by
Grafiche Veneziane s.c.r.l., Venice
for Marsilio Arte s.r.l., Venice

MIX
Paper | Supporting responsible forestry
FSC® C151617

Available through ARTBOOK | D.A.P.
75 Broad Street, Suite 630
New York, NY 10004
www.artbook.com

contents

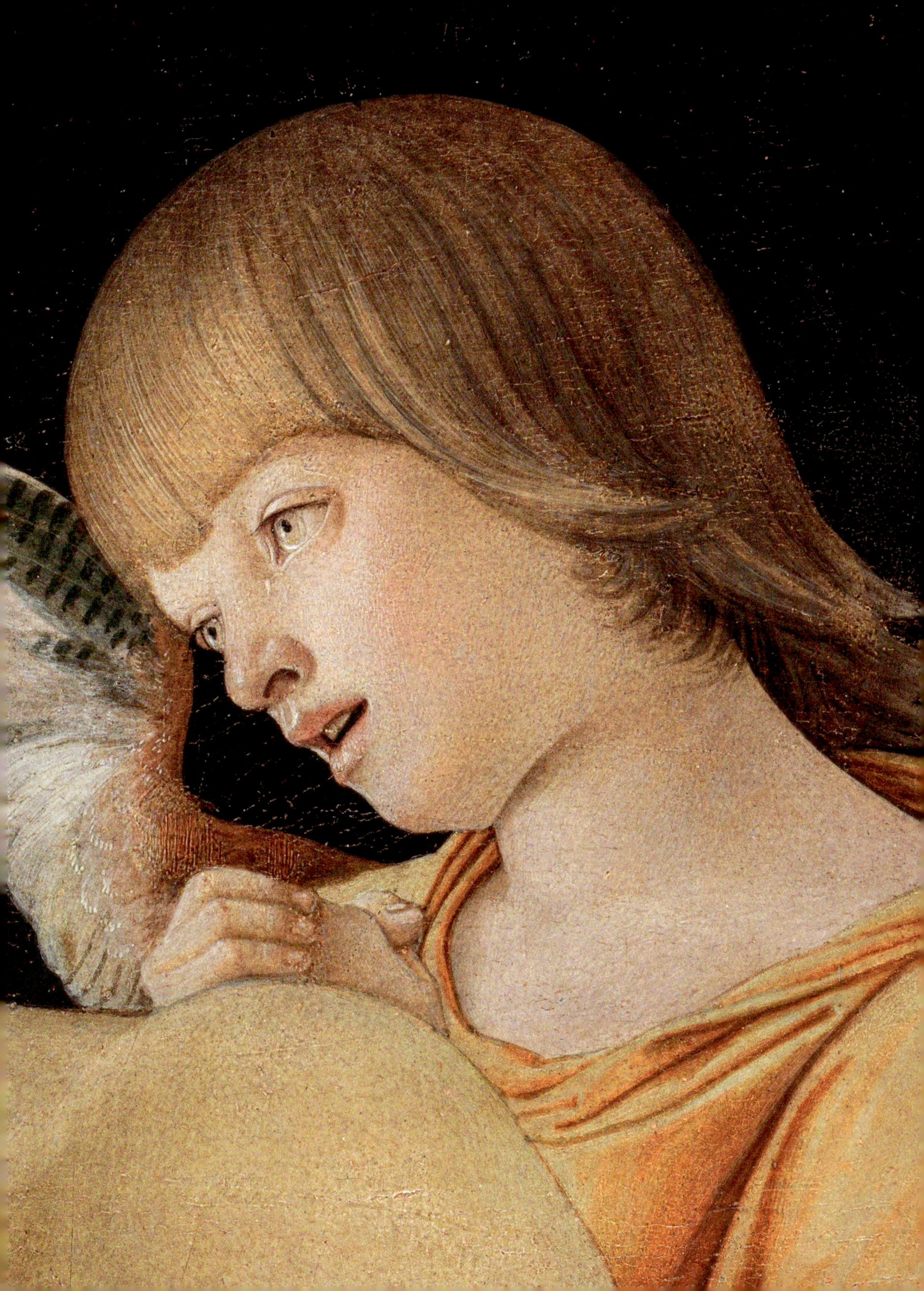

Introduction

Toto Bergamo Rossi

Venetian Heritage is an international nonprofit organization that for twenty-six years has supported cultural projects through conservation, exhibitions, publications, conferences, academic study, and research. The organization aims to increase awareness of the immense legacy of Venetian art in Italy and in those areas once part of the Republic of Venice. One of the most important projects supported in Venice, to cite only a few, has been the cleaning of the façades of the church of Gesuiti and the church of San Zaccaria, the latter being one of the finest examples of early Venetian Renaissance architecture. Venetian Heritage has also financed the restoration of the monumental staircase built by Mauro Codussi in the Scuola Grande San Giovanni Evangelista. Thanks to a fruitful collaboration with the Gallerie dell'Accademia, Venetian Heritage has financed the permanent installation in the first six rooms of the museum's new ground floor exhibition spaces and the restoration of several masterpieces, including *Il Castigo dei Serpenti* by Giambattista Tiepolo. In Padua, Venetian Heritage has funded the restoration of the famous chapel of Saint Anthony in the Basilica of that same name. In Croatia, Venetian Heritage has financed the restoration of the façade of the Trogir Cathedral and the Orsini Chapel. Venetian Heritage has also financed the restoration of the magnificent façade of the Cathedral of Saint Mark on Korcula, a Dalmatian island that was part of the Republic of Venice from 1200 to the fall of the Serenissima in 1797.

In the past decade, Venetian Heritage has enhanced its reach through a series of interventions designed not only to preserve important masterpieces of Venetian art but also to support and expand a number of Venetian National museums. Projects include the renovation of the

Palazzo Grimani Museum, which saw the return of the original sculpture collection after 400 years, and the ongoing restoration and restyling of the Galleria Giorgio Franchetti alla Ca' d'Oro. At the Ca' d'Oro, Venetian Heritage also organized and financed the 2022 exhibition *From Donatello To Alessandro Vittoria 1450–1600, 150 Years of Sculpture in the Republic of Venice*. As part of its engagement in cultural heritage promotion and cooperation between public institutions and private entities, Venetian Heritage has financed the restoration of Giovanni Bellini's *Pietà* (*Dead Christ supported by Four Angels*), a masterpiece of the early Venetian Renaissance kept in the Museo della Città di Rimini "Luigi Tonini". The conservation history of the *Pietà* is complex and layered: from the first restoration carried out by Mauro Pellicioli in 1929 to the 1969 intervention by Ottorino Nonfarmale and Otello Caprara, to the recently completed restoration by CBC – Conservazione Beni Culturali, thanks to which we can finally admire once again Bellini's brilliant original colors.

With tha aim of promoting Venetian art and making it accessible to as many people as possible, Venetian Heritage has decided to organize an exhibition entirely dedicated to Bellini's *Pietà* and its restoration. The first venue for the exhibition is the Galleria Giorgio Franchetti alla Ca' d'Oro in Venice, where the *Pietà* is exceptionally shown alongside Andrea Mantegna's *San Sebastiano*, one of the museum's masterpieces. The presence of both works allows for an unprecedented exploration of two different figurative languages. Furthermore, significance to this evocative juxtaposition is provided by the special relationship between the two artists. In 1453, Andrea Mantegna married Giovanni Bellini's sister Nicolosia and became a member of the most important family of painters in Venice of the time, which also included Giovanni's father, Iacopo, and his brother, Gentile. Bellini's *Pietà* will subsequently be exhibited at the celebrated Morgan Library & Museum in New York, in an exhibition especially dedicated to it. At the end of the exhibition tour, the *Pietà* will return home to the Museo della Città di Rimini

"Luigi Tonini", where it will once again be exceptionally exhibited alongside Mantegna's *San Sebastiano* from the Ca' d'Oro. The presence of the two works will also be the occasion to highlight the cultural exchanges and artistic influences between the two Adriatic cities of Venice and Rimini in the second half of the fifteenth century. This project represents yet another example of productive synergy between public and private sectors: a fruitful collaboration between the Museo della Città di Rimini "Luigi Tonini", the Direzione regionale Musei nazionali Veneto—through the Galleria Giorgio Franchetti alla Ca' d'Oro—and Venetian Heritage. A great initiative based on a shared vision focused on the protection and promotion of the priceless Venetian cultural heritage, which will open new possibilities for the furthering of the knowledge, appreciation, and diffusion of Venetian and Italian art around the world.

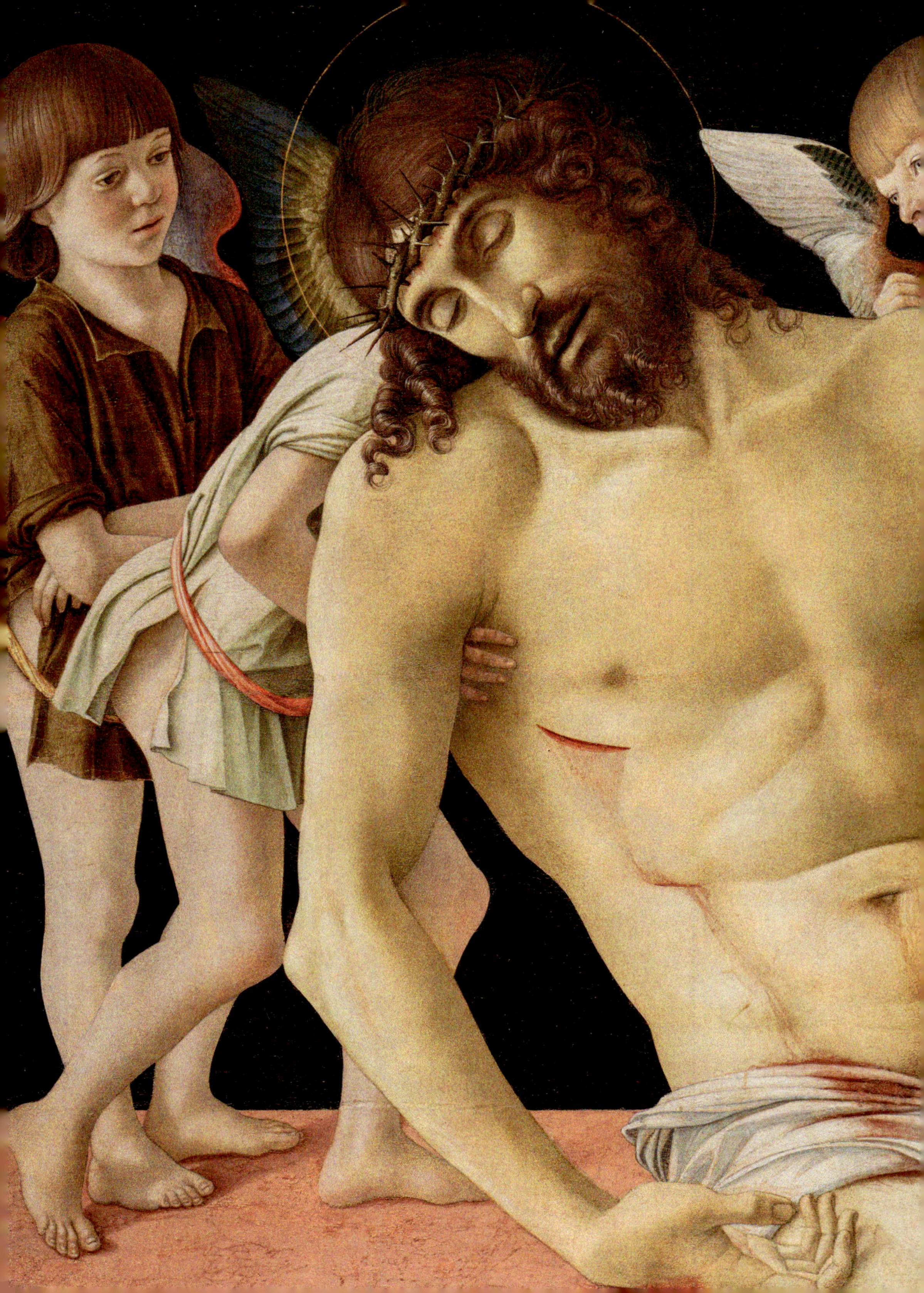

Giovanni Bellini: "Imago Domini Nostri Iesu Christi Salvatoris . . . in Formam Pietatis"

Peter Humfrey

At an unknown date between 1805 and 1851, Giovanni Bellini's (circa 1438/1440–1516) *Pietà* (*Dead Christ supported by Four Angels*) was transferred from the church of San Francesco in Rimini—better known by its sobriquet of the Tempio Malatestiano—into the custody of the local Comune.[1] The painting had been in the church for some three centuries, ever since the death in 1499 of its likely commissioner, Rainerio di Lodovico Migliorati, counsellor to the ruling Malatesta family, and a prominent figure in Riminese politics and culture in the last third of the fifteenth century.[2] An inscription in small Gothic minuscules on the pink ledge at the bottom right reads 'Ioannes Bellinus pingebat'; and although this is most unlikely to be the artist's own signature, it is certainly early, and may even have been applied by the patron.[3] To judge from the style, dimensions and iconography, Migliorati had ordered it from Bellini in Venice in about 1470, and had kept it as a stimulus to private devotion in his palace, before instructing in his will that it be placed in a projected funerary chapel in the church of Sant'Antonio. This small church, or oratory, was situated alongside that of San Francesco and was officiated by the same congregation of Franciscan friars; and it seems that from the beginning the patron's executors decided instead to place the painting in the larger and more prestigious building. The painting is in any case likely to be identical with the one by Bellini recorded in San Francesco by Giorgio Vasari in the first edition of the *Vite* of 1550, and then in the revised edition of 1568.[4] Local sources in the seventeenth and eighteenth centuries, namely Raffaele Adimari (1616) and Carlo Francesco Marcheselli (1754), later recorded it in the church's sacristy.[5]

Vasari's account raises a number of difficult problems, but before confronting these, it is worth looking more closely at the painting itself, which is now universally regarded as one of the supreme masterpieces of the artist's early maturity. Dominating the composition is the naked and dead body of Christ, shown in half length, with the wounds of the nails in his hands and of the lance in his chest, and the Crown of Thorns on his head. In terms of the gospel narratives and of their traditional depiction in art, the appearance of Christ in this form refers to the interval between his deposition from the Cross by his disciples on Good Friday, and his Resurrection on Easter Sunday. Yet no particular moment in the story is represented; rather, this is a timeless image, devised with the purpose of providing the devout Christian with a visual stimulus to meditation on a divine mystery. The dead Christ is not accompanied by contemporary witnesses, but by a group of four child angels, who contemplate the marks of his suffering with expressions of gentle sorrow. Only one steps forwards to prevent the weight of his body from falling backwards; and this gesture, more symbolic than practical, reinforces the religious message that although Christ died on the Cross, he was to rise again on the third day. The pink ledge, while suggestive of the sarcophagus in which he was to be buried, simultaneously resembles an altar table, at which his self-sacrifice for the sake of mankind is constantly re-enacted in the sacrament of the Eucharist.

The mood of the painting, simultaneously of sorrow and consolation, is reinforced by the composition and pictorial handling, which at once vividly realistic and highly artificial. Many of the details are beautifully observed from life: the curling hairs of Christ's hair and beard; the softness of the children's skin; the coloured feathers of their wings, resembling those of birds; the sensuous, almost erotic way in which limb brushes against limb. Yet the figure composition, compressed within the narrow stage created by the foreground ledge, and set against a smooth dark foil, apparently of black marble, evokes sculpture in low relief rather than forms in the round. All reference to landscape, or to any other spatial surroundings, is suppressed. The heads are all on a level; arms and legs set up a pattern of silhouetted shapes; curves and angles answer one another. Similarly, the colours are carefully restricted to a range of pinks, ivories and olive greens, and their repetitions complement the decorative interlacing of the forms. The artist even introduces an element of visual wit in the way in which the head of the second angel from the left disappears behind that of the Saviour, while the curve of his wing corresponds exactly to that of Christ's head and halo, and even conveys an effect of radiating light.

In art-historical terminology, this type of image—which has its ancestry in Byzantine art, and which in Venice had an authoritative prototype in Paolo Veneziano's *pala feriale* above the high altar of San Marco (1345)—is known alternatively as a *Pietà* and as a *Man of Sorrows*. The latter term has the advantage of distinguishing it clearly from another type of image, in which the Dead Christ is shown stretched across the lap of the full-length, seated figure of the grieving Virgin Mary. This other type, although famous above all from the sculptural group by Michelangelo in St Peter's in the Vatican, was also adopted by Bellini, in his very slightly later Donà dalle Rose *Pietà* of circa 1502 (Gallerie dell'Accademia, Venice). But confusingly or not, the term *Pietà* remains in frequent use for the type of image represented by the present work, in which the Dead Christ is shown in half length and vertically (or at least, seated and leaning), and usually accompanied by two or more mourners. Indeed, such use of the term has ample historical justification, as is illustrated by two documents of 1499 referring to the Rimini painting itself: the will of Rainerio Migliorati, written in Latin, in which he calls it a "tabulam depictam manu Iohannis Bellini, in qua est depicta imago domini nostri Iesu Christi Salvatoris mortui et sublate de cruce in formam pietatis"; and the testator's inventory, in which it is itemised in very similar words in the vulgate as "una ancona o vero taula dove è dep(i)nta la imagine del N.S.Iesu Christo in forma de pietà, descesa de la croce."[6]

From these references it is clear that although Migliorati wanted his painting to be placed in his mortuary chapel after his death, it was previously in his private possession. The term 'ancona' may accordingly be understood in its literal sense, simply as a pictorial image, not as an altarpiece made for display above a church altar. It is true that in the fifteenth century, following the

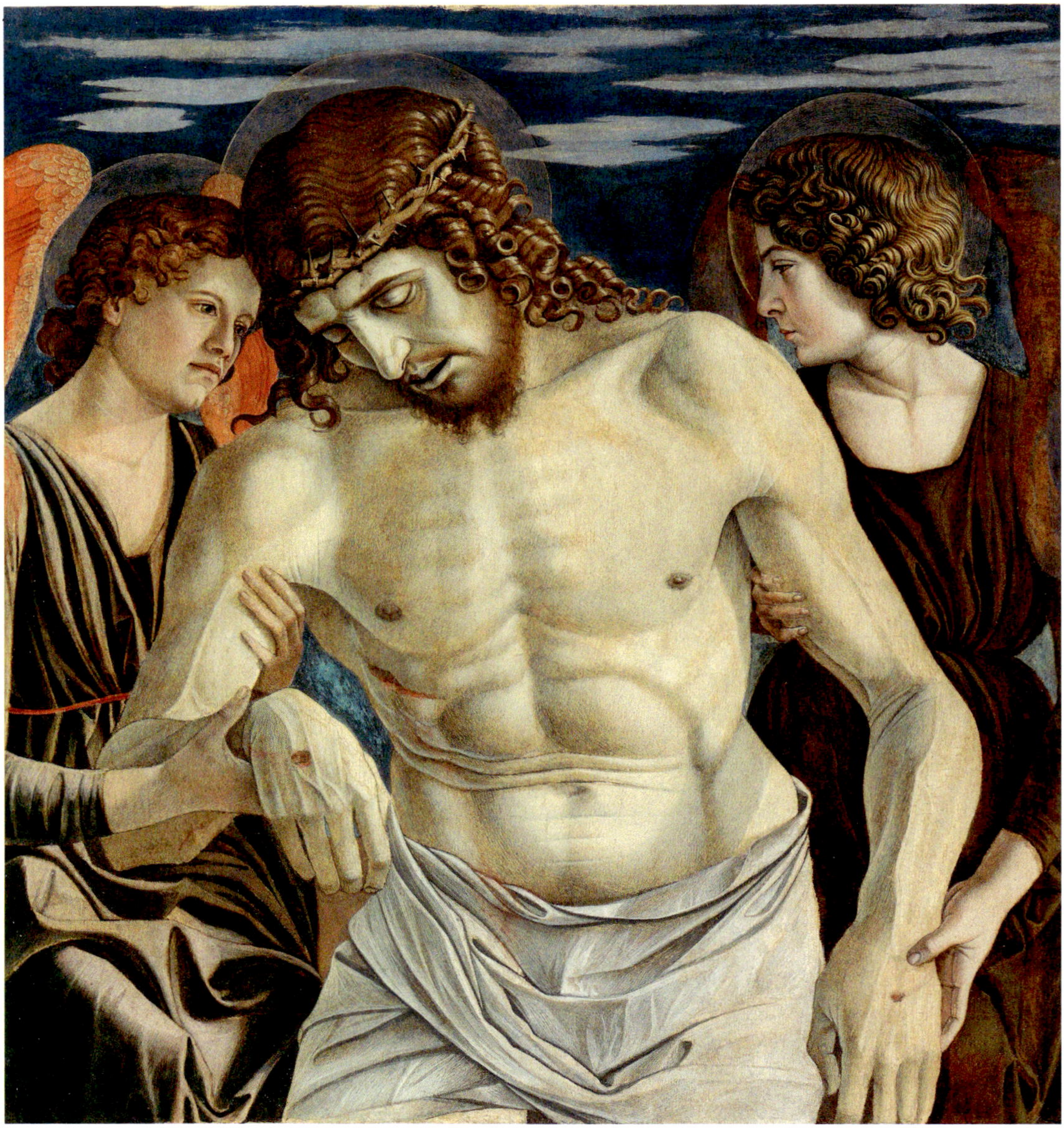

1
Giovanni Bellini, *Pietà with two Angels* (pinnacle of *Saint Vincent Ferrer* polyptych), circa 1465–1468, panel, 74.4 × 66.8 cm, Venice, Church of Santi Giovanni e Paolo

2
Giovanni Bellini, *Pietà with Joseph of Arimathea, Nicodemus and Saint Mary Magdalen* (former pinnacle of the *Coronation of the Virgin* in Pesaro), circa 1475–1476, panel, 107 × 84 cm, Rome, Pinacoteca Vaticana (inv. no. 40290)

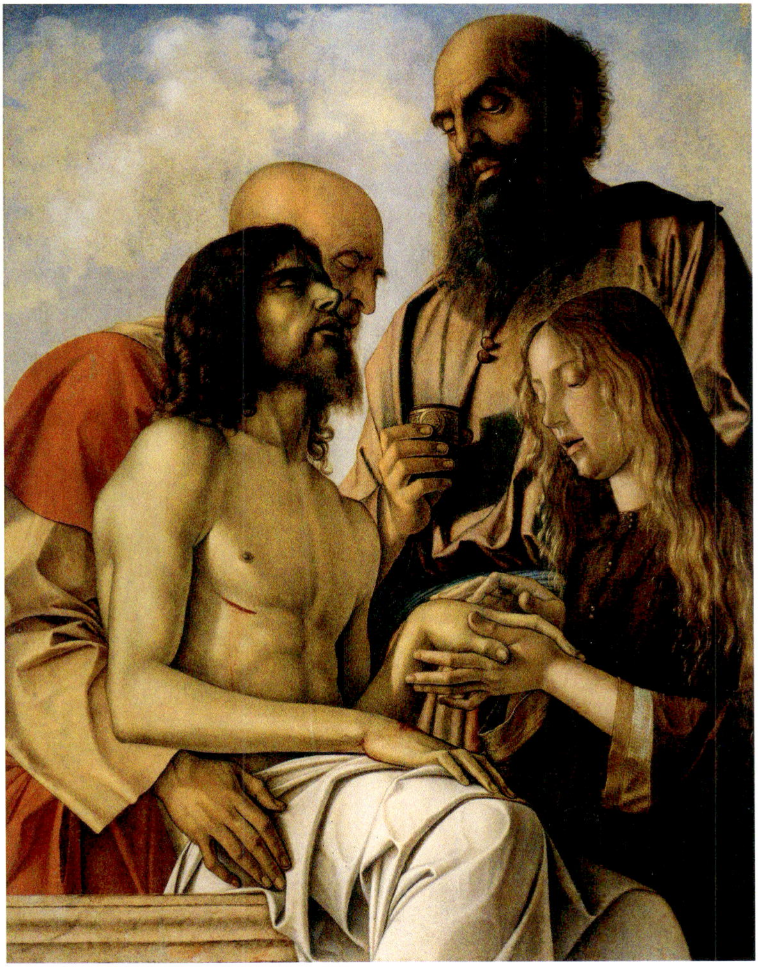

prototype by Paolo Veneziano in San Marco, this iconography was frequently employed for altarpieces; but in such cases, it was placed at the apex of a polyptych—as by Bellini himself for his *Saint Vincent Ferrer* polyptych still in place in Santi Giovanni e Paolo in Venice (fig. 1), or for his *Coronation of the Virgin* in San Francesco, Pesaro (fig. 2)—and never for the main panel, in which the figures were customarily depicted on a larger scale and in full length, as in representations of the closely related subjects of the Deposition and the Lamentation. A rare example of a hybrid iconography is represented by the painter's *Pietà with Saints Mark and Nicholas*, executed in 1472 for the private chapel of the doge in Palazzo Ducale (fig. 3).[7] Although in this case the

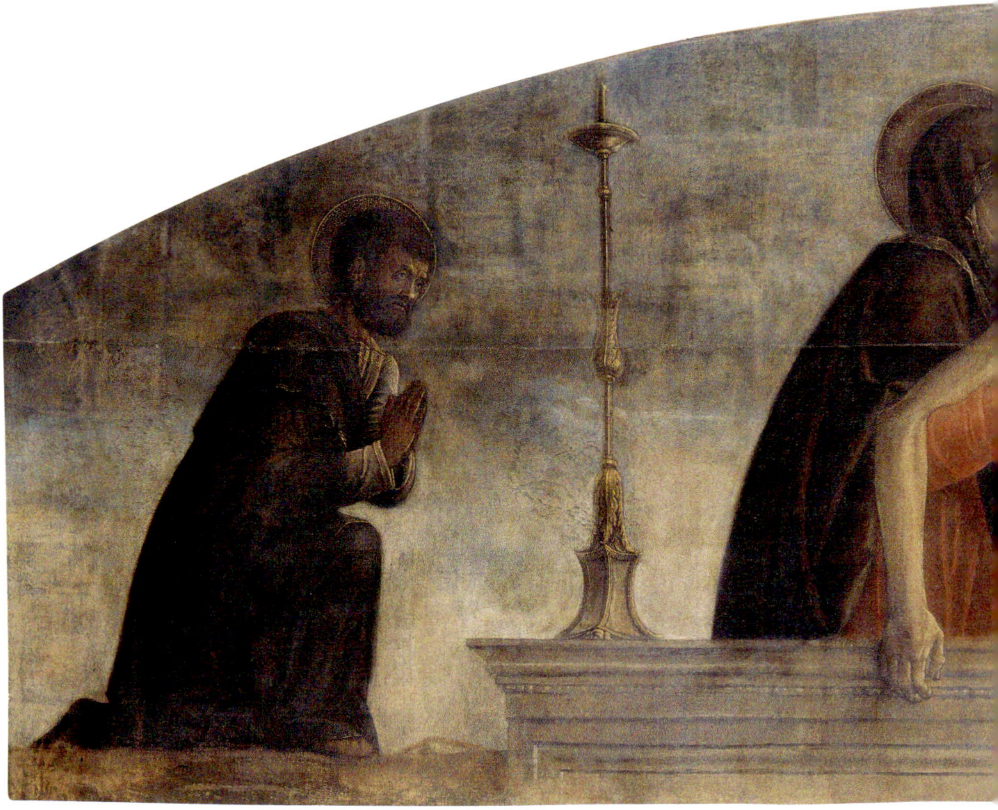

3
Giovanni Bellini, *Pietà with the Virgin and Saint John, and Saints Mark and Nicholas,* 1472, canvas, 116 × 319 cm, signed: "IOHANES. BELLINVS", Venice, Doge's Palace (inv. TS p.l. n. 48 n. 433)

white marble structure above which Christ, the Virgin and Saint John appear strongly resembles an altar—a resemblance that is further enhanced by the liturgical candles, and the kneeling saints at the sides—the lunette-shaped format of the painting implies that it was not placed directly above the real altar of the chapel, but much higher, under the vault of its architecture.

In general, it may be assumed that Bellini's many variations of the theme of the *Pietà*, or *Man of Sorrows*—whether relatively large or relatively small—were painted for private devotion, in the context of the owner's home. Perhaps they were usually placed in his bedroom, perhaps above a prie-dieu for intense spiritual contemplation, or else simply on the wall. But

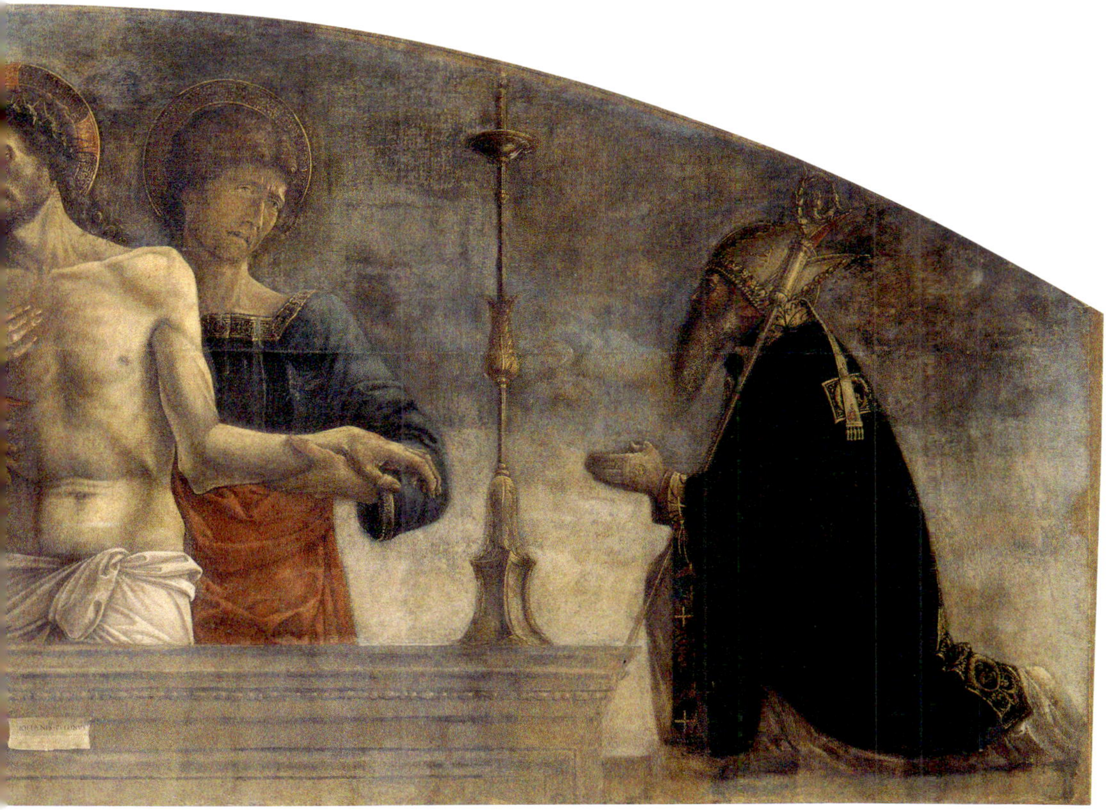

they may well instead have been placed in a more public room in the house, where their aesthetic beauty could be more easily admired by the owner's friends. Either way, it is likely that the many examples of the type were not originally destined for any particular position; indeed, a large part of their attraction for patrons must have been the fact that they were appropriate for different domestic spaces, and could even be moved from the home to a church. Indeed, in the case of the present work, it cannot be excluded that already when ordering his painting, Migliorati intended it to be displayed after his death in close proximity to his sepulchre: on the wall of his chapel; or perhaps even as a frontal, or antependium, for his altar.[8]

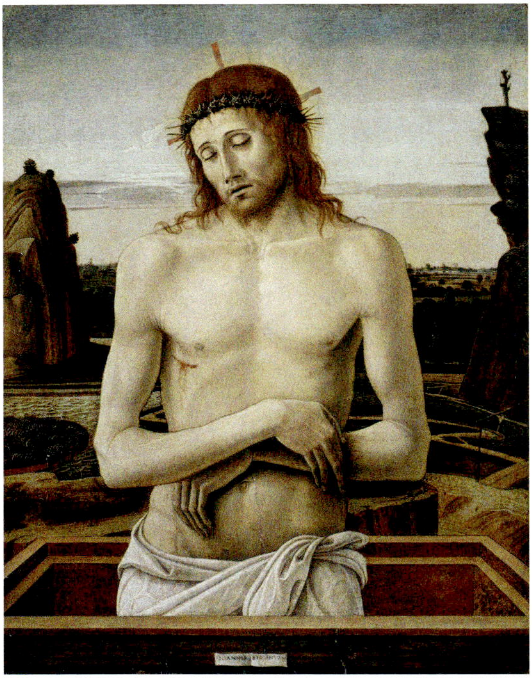

4
Giovanni Bellini, *Pietà*, circa 1464–66, panel, 50.5 × 40.4 cm, Milan, Museo Poldi Pezzoli (inv. no. 1587)

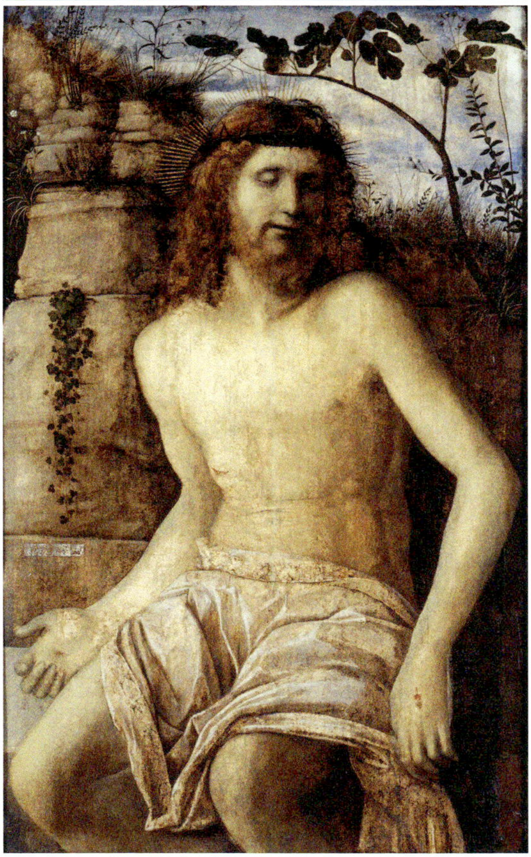

5
Giovanni Bellini, *Pietà*, circa 1510, panel, 107 × 70 cm, Stockholm, Nationalmuseum (inv. no. 1726)

6
Giovanni Bellini, *Pietà with the Virgin and Saint John,* circa 1468–1470, panel, 86 × 107 cm, Milan, Pinacoteca di Brera (Reg. cron. 228)

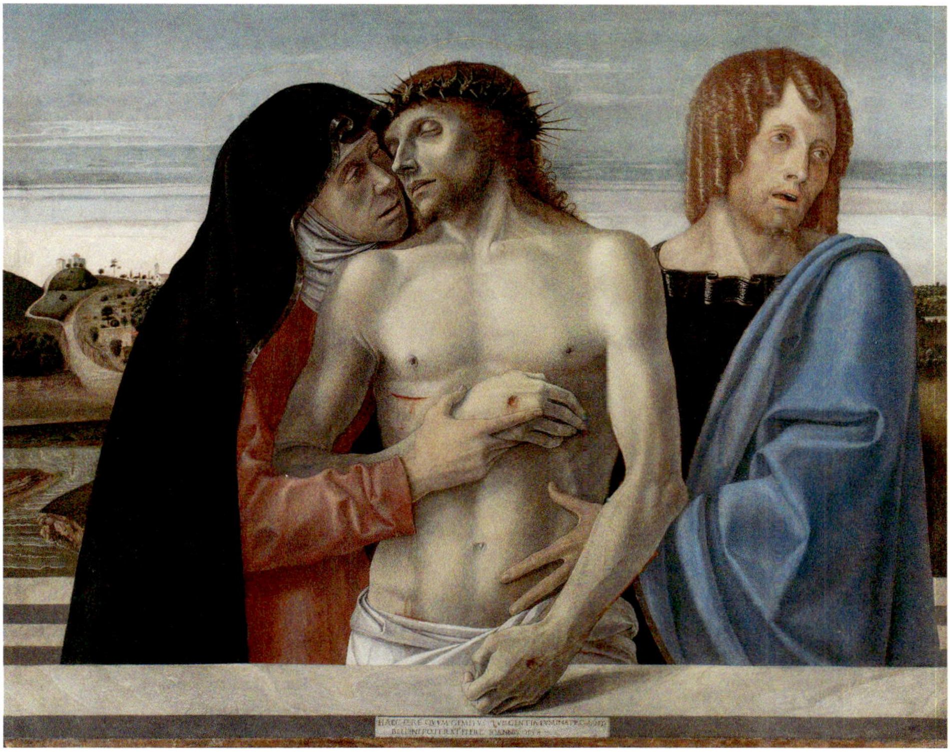

Together with that of the Virgin and Child, the *Pietà* was the subject pursued by Bellini most frequently, and with the greatest expressive commitment, throughout his long career.[9] One of the earliest, probably dating from the early 1460s is the little panel in the Museo Poldi Pezzoli, in which Christ is seen in waist length, standing alone (fig. 4); probably the last is the much larger panel of circa 1507–10 in Stockholm, in which he is still alone, but is seen seated in knee length (fig. 5). In the many variations painted in the intervening half century, however, Christ is almost always accompanied by mourners, whether the Virgin and Saint John—the figures traditionally shown beside the Cross in scenes of the Crucifixion—or angels. Examples of the former cast of figures include the paintings in the Accademia Carrara, Bergamo, and the Pinacoteca di Brera (fig. 6), as well as that in Palazzo Ducale; examples of the latter, besides the present work, include those in the Museo Correr (fig. 7), in London (fig. 8), and in Berlin (Gemäldegalerie). While these differences do not fundamentally alter the

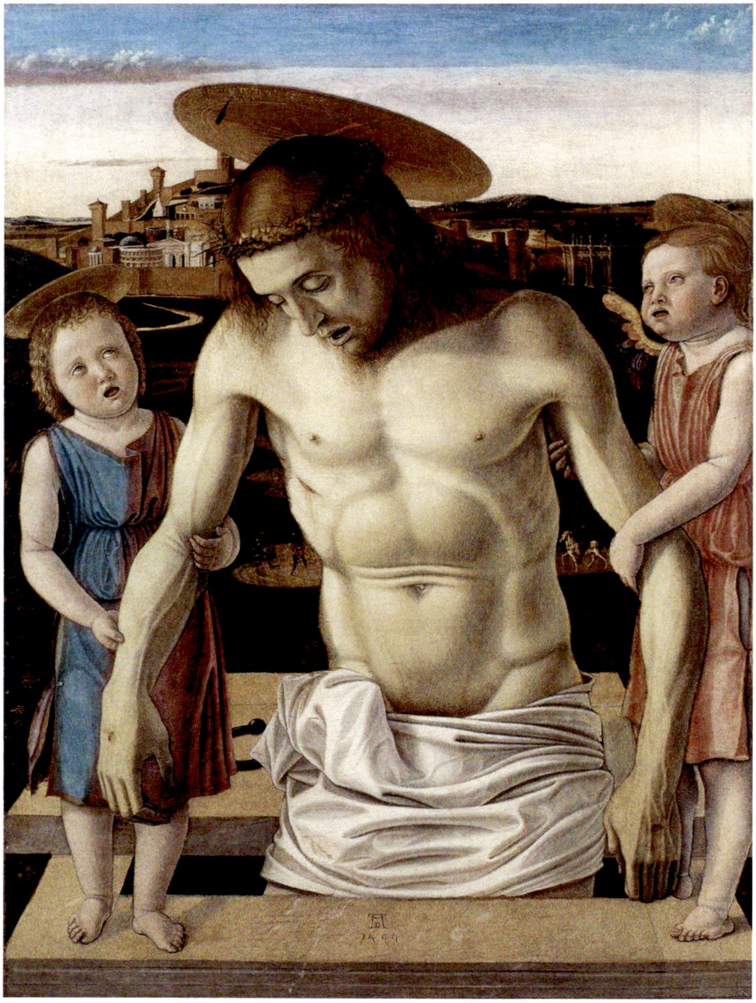

7
Giovanni Bellini, *Pietà with two Angels,*
circa 1466–1468, panel, 64.5 × 50 cm,
Venice, Museo Civico Correr
(inv. no. cl. I. 39)

religious message of the image, they do sometimes involve a subtle difference of emphasis; and whereas the presence of historical mourners relates the scene more explicitly to the tragedy of Good Friday, their replacement by angels—celestial beings who serve God in heaven—shifts the emphasis to the timeless, sacramental possibility of human redemption.

The great majority of Bellini's representations of the *Pietà* are datable to the 1460s and early 1470s, the period of the painter's closest preoccupation

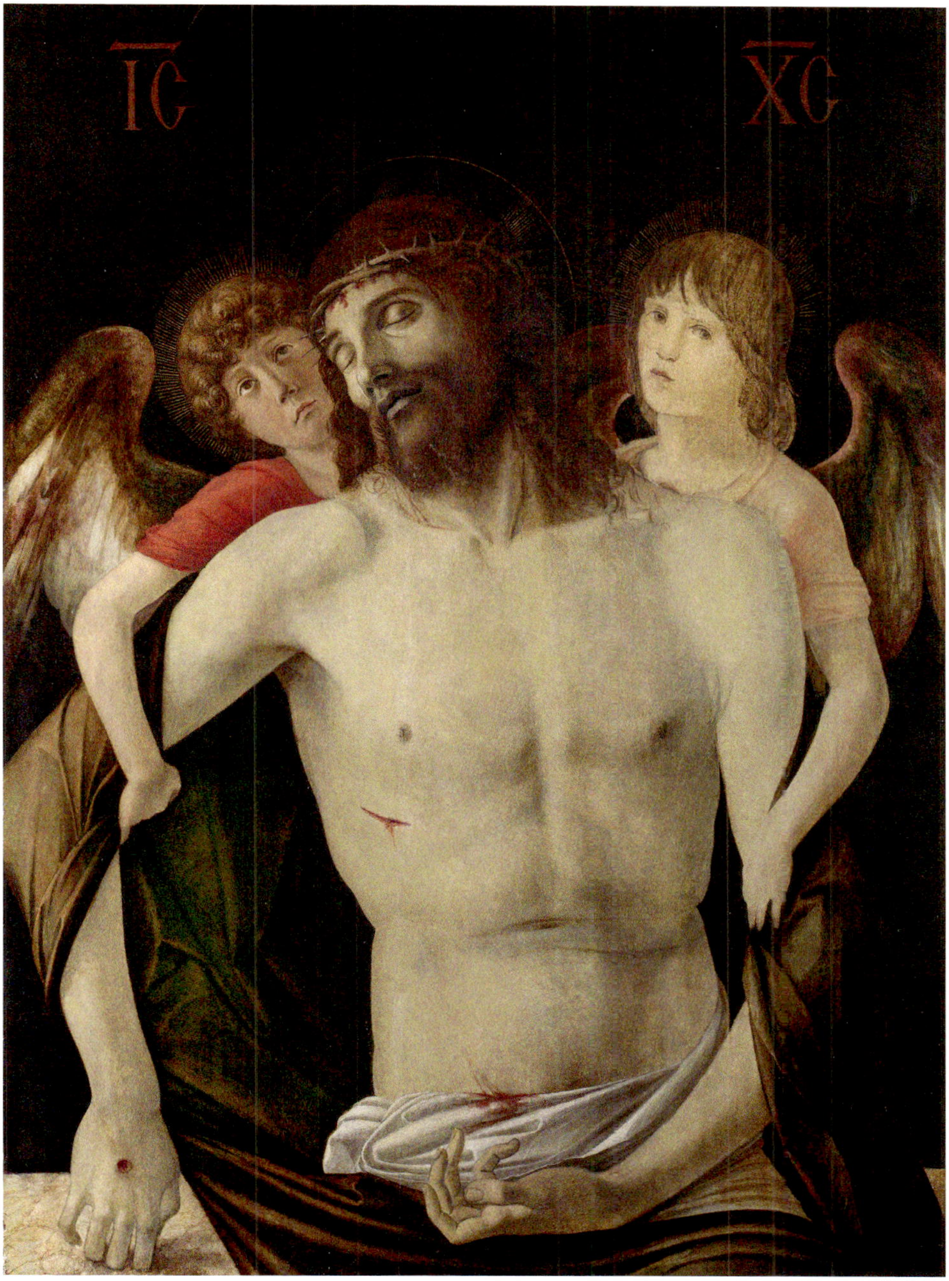

8
Giovanni Bellini, *Pietà with two Angels*, circa 1470–1475, panel, 95 × 71.7 cm, London, National Gallery (inv. no. NG3912)

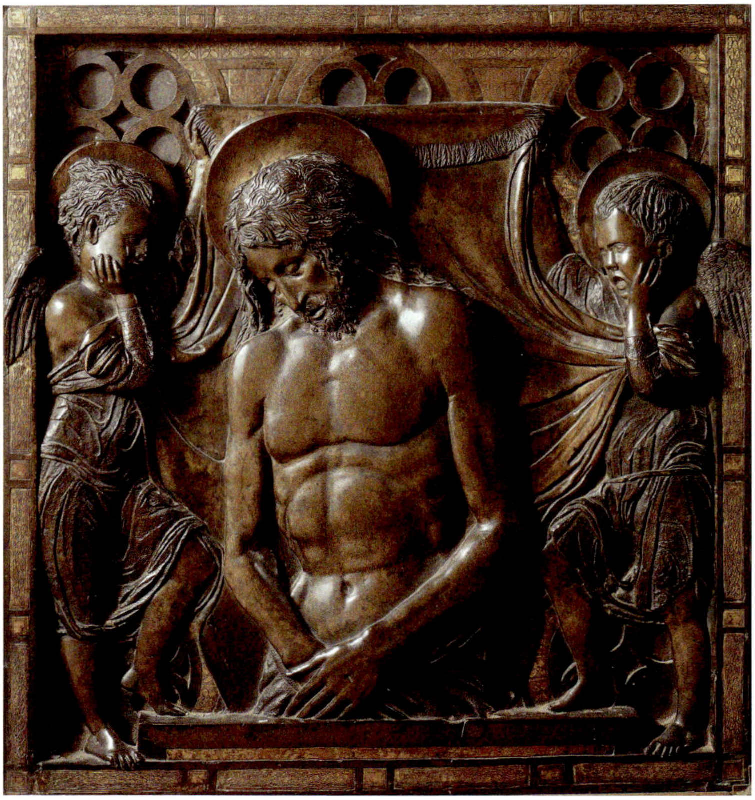

9
Donatello, *Pietà with two Angels*,
circa 1446–1450, bronze, 58 × 56 cm,
Padua, Basilica del Santo

with recent developments in Padua: notably by his brother-in-law, Andrea Mantegna, but also with the work on the high altar of the Santo by Donatello. The impact of the sculptor's bronze *Pietà with two Angels* (fig. 9) is particularly evident in the Bellini's version in the Museo Correr, both in its composition and in its emotional charge; but strong echoes of the relief continue to reverberate in the present painting in Rimini. More difficult to assess is the relationship between the latter and a marble *Pietà with Five Angels* in the Victoria and Albert Museum (fig. 10). This has traditionally been associated with Donatello, and has been dated to various moments in his career, including to his early periods in Florence and Rome. A case has recently even been made that it is not by Donatello at all, but by an early sixteenth-century imitator.[10] But Rimini *Pietà* resembles the sculpture

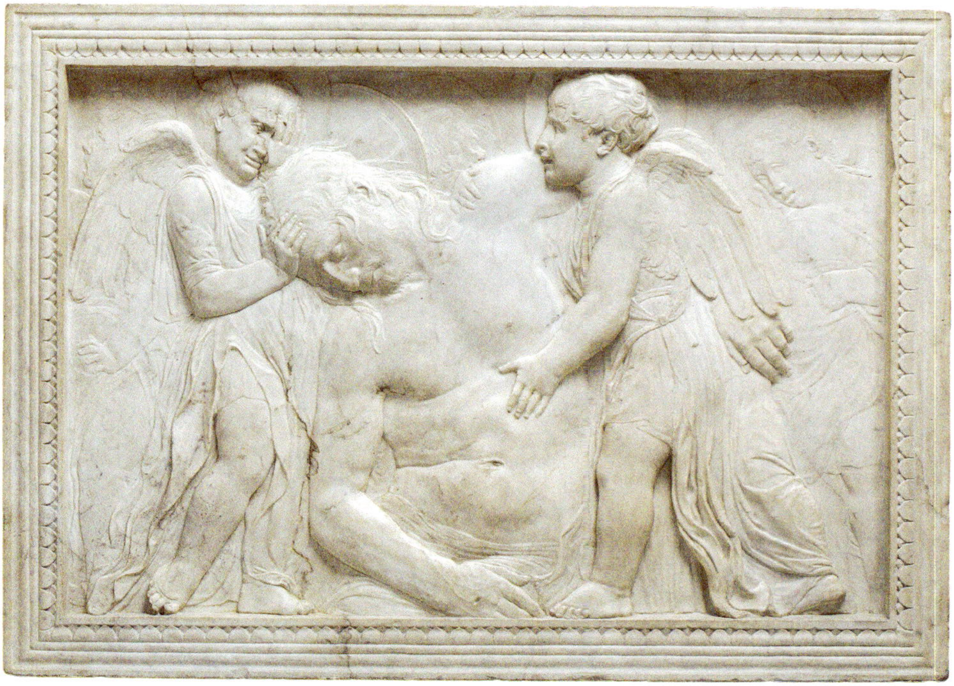

10
Donatello and assistant, *Pietà with Five Angels*, circa 1450 (?), marble, 80.5 × 114.3 cm, London, Victoria and Albert Museum (inv. no. 7577–1861)

so closely in a number of ways—in its near-identical size, in its broad format, in the emphasis on shallow relief, and in the additional angels, one of whose faces is hidden—that it seems inconceivable that Bellini did not know it, and that it therefore probably dates from Donatello's ten-year stay in Padua between 1443 and 1453.

Testimony to the painter's continuing preoccupation with the subject of the *Pietà* is provided by another variation in Berlin, and by the grisaille in the Uffizi, both of circa 1490; indeed, his ability to rethink it, investing it with never-ceasing changes of mood, composition, and pictorial style, is nothing short of miraculous. Of all these many examples, however, only that in Palazzo Ducale has a documented date—and even this has been doubted, because the inscription 1472 once recorded on the canvas is no longer visible. Otherwise, datings of individual works depend on different readings by scholars of Bellini's early stylistic development, and this matter remains controversial, largely because of the continuing uncertainty about his birthdate, and about his age relative to that of Mantegna. Such controversies, however, relate above all to the earliest works, and there is growing consensus that the present *Pietà* from Rimini dates from the first half of the 1470s:[11] that is to say, in a phase when, although the contours of Bellini's forms remain sharply linear, they show a simplification and relaxation compared with those of Mantegna, and softer internal modelling, particularly in areas of the flesh. This is the phase, too, in which Bellini had begun to abandon the traditional technique of egg tempera, and is experimenting with oil painting, as also seen in the stylistically and emotionally very similar *Pietà with two Angels* in London.[12] In these respects, the present work may be contrasted with the work that is generally recognised as the most powerful and spiritually intense of all the painter's variations on the theme—as well as the one most ambitious in its scale—the great *Pietà with the Virgin and Saint John*—in the Pinacoteca di Brera. Although variously dated by scholars from the mid 1460s to the early 1470s,[13] this work is usually and rightly seen as stylistically and technically close to the *Saint Vincent Ferrer* polyptych, which for external, circumstantial reasons is datable to circa 1465–68, and in which the incisive, chiselled forms inspired by Mantegna similarly remain more pronounced than in the painting from Rimini. Compared with the undulating compositional rhythms of the latter, the Brera *Pietà* is structured on a rigid grid of verticals and horizontals, and the treatment of the musculature and the draperies is more explicitly sculptural, an effect that is further emphasised by the dry precision of the egg medium. While these differences of composition and handling serve to complement the differences of mood in the two paintings—the one expressing an intense and bitter grief, and the other a tender compassion—they also help confirm that the Rimini *Pietà* is also slightly later.

Some scholars, detecting the influence of Antonello da Messina in the present work, have dated it later still, to the second half of the decade, after the visit by the Sicilian to Venice in 1475–76, and also after the completion by Bellini at around the same time of his great *Coronation of the Virgin* in Pesaro. Comparison, however, between the Rimini *Pietà* and the version of the subject originally placed at the pinnacle of the altarpiece (fig. 2) does not support this argument. By contrast with the composition of the Rimini painting, with its frieze-like arrangement of overlapping planes, that of the pinnacle is emphatically three-dimensional, with four fully-rounded figures occupying clearly-defined positions in space. The stereometric effect is further enhanced by Bellini's growing mastery of the oil medium, which he exploits to convey more gradual transitions from light to shade. This is the direction in which his art was to develop in the years that immediately followed, towards the achievement of the *San Giobbe Altarpiece*, datable to circa 1480 (Gallerie dell'Accademia, Venice), and away from the moment represented by the Rimini *Pietà*. Further confirmation that the latter was painted in the early 1470s are its stylistic similarities to works for which there exists external evidence for a date in this phase: the *Portrait of a Boy* in Birmingham (fig. 11); the *Jörg Fugger* (Norton Simon Museum, Pasadena); and the *Saint Justina* (Fondazione Bagatti Valsecchi, Milan). Probably also closely contemporary was another monumental work representing the Virgin and Child with Saints, the *Saint Catherine of Siena Altarpiece*, the composition of which was recorded in an engraving before the painting was tragically destroyed by fire in Santi Giovanni e Paolo in 1867.

The probably somewhat earlier Brera *Pietà* is exceptional among Bellini's works in that the *cartellino* on the foreground parapet carries a two-line Latin inscription derived from the *Elegies* of the pre-Christian poet Propertius, and declaring that the artist communicates such a deep sense of sorrow at Christ's death that the painting itself seems to shed tears. This reworking of a phrase from a classical author to create an elaborate conceit in praise of the expressive power of Bellini's art implies a patron of sophisticated humanist learning. Unfortunately, however, his identity is unknown, and the present painting from Rimini is, in fact, the only one in this series of representations of the subject for which there is any evidence about who commissioned it. Although this evidence dates from a quarter of a century after the likely date of the painting's execution, and in theory it cannot be excluded that during this period it had already changed hands, it remains overwhelmingly likely that the original owner was the same courtier and humanist who still owned it at the time of his death in 1499: Rainerio di Lodovico Migliorati.

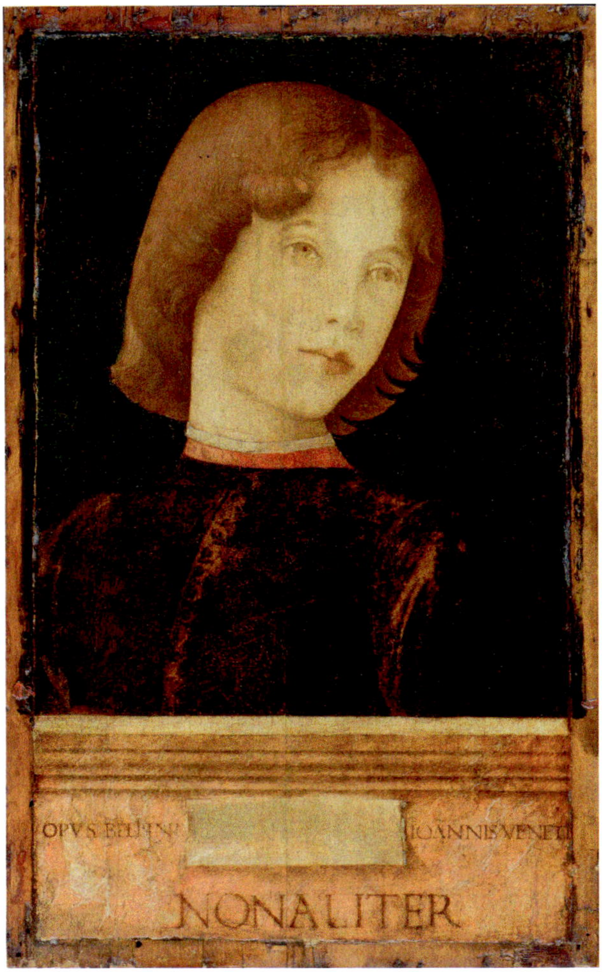

11
Giovanni Bellini, *Portrait of a Boy (Giovanni Andrea Probi?)*, circa 1474, panel, 38 × 23 cm, Barber Institute of Fine Arts, University of Birmingham (inv. no. 46.11)

Too little is known about this person for him to have earned an entry in the *Dizionario Biografico degli Italiani*; indeed, virtually all biographical information about him has to be gleaned from his will and from an inventory of his possessions, published and discussed in 1962 by the distinguished historian and philologist Augusto Campana.[14] Described as "magnificus ac clarissimus legum doctor", Migliorati was counsellor at the end of his life to the last ruler of the Malatesta dynasty, Pandolfo IV; and his intimacy with the family is reflected in the fact that one of his executors was Violante Bentivoglio, Pandolfo's wife. Migliorati was the owner of an extensive library, comprising manuscripts on secular and canon law, philosophy, poetry and warfare, all of which he left to the convent of San Francesco. He was in close contact with other Riminese humanists such as Roberto Valturio (1405–1475) and Roberto Orsi (circa 1420–1496), and calls the latter his "carissimo amico"—suggesting, perhaps, that he was of about the same age. Further evidence of his friendship with the latter is provided by an epigram addressed to him by Orsi, which mentions that Migliorati had given him had given him a collection of ancient Roman coins in return for a gift of a marble head.[15] The inventory lists further ancient sculpture, coins and "pedre intagliate", as well as books of devotion and two "anconette de Nostra Donna".

His choice of the adjoining oratory of Sant'Antonio as his burial site further reflects his close association with the Tempio Malatestiano and its surrounding complex.[16] Apart from the will, he is known to have been sent by Pandolfo on a diplomatic mission to Venice in 1496; and in 1482 he is recorded in connection with the favoured Malatesta painter, Piero della Francesca. In April of that year Migliorati facilitated the twelve-month rent by the painter of a house and garden in Rimini, presumably to enable him to undertake an otherwise undocumented commission, perhaps a fresco for the current ruler, Pandolfo's father Roberto.[17] In the present state of knowledge, further biographical details remain a matter of speculation; but if he was indeed a close contemporary of his friend Roberto Orsi, Migliorati may well have already been prominent at the court of the great Sigismondo Malatesta (died 1468). It is also easy to imagine, given the close contacts with the Republic of Venice under both Sigismondo and Roberto, that the counsellor made other official trips to Venice before that of 1496, including in about 1470, when he could have made personal contact with Bellini. In this connection, it is interesting that in his will, unusually for the period, he gives the name of the painter when mentioning his devotional image: "Imago domini nostri Iesu Christi ... in formam pietatis ... manu Iohannis Bellini." In other words, like the anonymous commissioner of the slightly earlier painting in the Brera, Migliorati clearly valued his *Pietà* not merely for its subject and for its function as an aid to religious devotion, but as a work of art by the hand of a great painter.

It is perhaps not surprising that the association between the Rimini *Pietà* and Migliorati was forgotten after his death for four and a half centuries until the documents were published by Campana in 1962. It was certainly not known to Vasari, who when publishing the first edition of the *Vite* in 1550, unambiguously declared that the work was commissioned by Sigismondo Malatesta. In the same passage Vasari added another source of confusion for future art historians, when he described the painting as depicting just two "puttini"; while in the 1568 edition, instead of correcting this number, specified that the work was "un quadro grande." It has often been pointed out that all three of these misleading remarks are all the more surprising considering that the artist-writer had visited Rimini in person as recently as 1548, both to collect material for his book, and to undertake altarpiece commissions not only for the church of Santa Maria della Scolca, but also for San Francesco itself. The problem of how to interpret Vasari's comments are discussed in fuller detail by Giovanni Sassu in the present publication; but something should also be said here in the spirit of *mea culpa*. In my recent book on Giovanni Bellini I attempted to reconcile two of Vasari's comments—on the patronage, and on the number of child angels—by suggesting that Migliorati's *Pietà* was preceded in the mid-1460s by one for Sigismondo, possibly identical with the painting in the Museo Correr, which not only depicts just two angels, but which, exceptionally for Bellini, includes a cityscape with antique buildings, which could be interpreted as an allusion to the classical origins of the city of Rimini.[18] But all this is to place too much trust in the understandable assumption by Vasari that an important fifteenth-century painting in the Tempio Malatestiano was commissioned by its builder, a famous Renaissance prince and munificent patron of the arts. Furthermore, as already pointed out by Campana, it is highly unlikely that if there were two paintings by Bellini in the church rather than just one, Vasari would have failed to notice.

Certainly Adimari (1616) mentions only one, as does Marcheselli (1754), who explicitly refers to Vasari's description, repeating his assertion of a commission by Sigismondo, while avoiding the question of the number of angels by referring simply to "alcuni Angioletti." Likewise, at the time on the Napoleonic suppressions, only one painting by Bellini was transferred from the church into the possession of the Comune. The attribution of this to the master has always been accepted, except—surprisingly and inexplicably—by Crowe and Cavalcaselle (1871), who reassigned it to Francesco Zaganelli.[19] Subsequent art historians, however, have been consistent in regarding it as one of Bellini's greatest achievements. The *fortuna critica* of the painting during the course of the twentieth century is the subject of the essay by Giulio Zavatta in the present publication, and need be sketched only briefly here. But in general, it may be said that scholars have been preoccupied with three interconnected issues: how to interpret the confusing account by Vasari; how to interpret the iconography, particularly in relation to the painter's other treatments of the subject; and above all, how to date the work. Already in 1914 Roberto Longhi dismissed Vasari's account of the patronage, pointing out that Sigismondo Malatesta died in 1468, far too early to have commissioned the painting, which Longhi (at that time) regarded as postdating the Pesaro *Coronation*.[20] Both before and after Campana's article of 1962, scholars have sought other ways of accommodating Vasari's remark: Pietro Paoletti (1929), for example, pointed out that in 1480 Sigismondo's illegitimate son and heir, the condottiero Roberto Malatesta, was admitted to the Scuola Grande di San Marco, where Bellini was also a member;[21] and even if for the majority of scholars this date too late to be directly relevant for the *Pietà*, Paoletti's observation introduced the possibility that the work was commissioned by Roberto rather than Sigismondo. Campana, too, when publishing the documents relating to Migliorati, did not exclude the possibility that the counsellor received the painting from a member of the Malatesta family, either Roberto or Pandolfo IV. Alternatively, according a different reading of Bellini's chronology, the *Pietà* could be dated to circa 1467–68, in which case Sigismondo could be recognised as Bellini's patron after all. But as has been argued above, the much more convincing dating to the early 1470s, apparently advanced for the first time by Carlo Gamba in 1937,[22] would exclude Sigismondo; and Campana's documents make the hypothesis of direct Malatesta patronage superfluous.

Campana's identification of Migliorati as the first known owner of the painting marked a major step forward not only in our understanding of its early history, but also in our knowledge of Bellini's circle of patrons in the period of his early maturity. For so important a figure in the history of Venetian—and European—painting, it is sobering to realise how little is known for certain of the origins of the great majority of his works, up to and including the *San Giobbe Altarpiece*. The identity of the patron not only of the Brera *Pietà*, but also of other early masterpieces such as the Correr *Transfiguration* and the London *Agony in the Garden*, not to mention all the early Madonnas, remains obscure; and before the mid-1480s any objective evidence for dates remains overwhelmingly circumstantial. Against this background, Campana's documents remain of exceptional interest. Yet as he himself admitted, they raise as many questions than they answer: they tell us little, for example, of the humanist-courtier's life before the moment of his death; they do not establish beyond all doubt that he was the original patron; and above all, they do nothing to confirm or deny the different datings assigned to the *Pietà* by art-historians on mainly visual evidence. But even though sixty years have passed since the publication of Campana's article, one may still hope that further research into the biography of Migliorati might one day clarify such matters, and tell us more about how Giovanni Bellini came to send one of his most beautiful, expressive and moving works to the city of Rimini.

1 For the fullest catalogue entry on the painting, with references to the vast bibliography up to 2017, see Mauro Lucco in *Giovanni Bellini: Catalogo Ragionato*, ed. by M. Lucco, Ponzano Veneto, 2019, pp. 375–77. More recent discussions include: K. Weick-Joch in *Mantegna and Bellini*, exhibition catalog (National Gallery, London, 1 October, 2018–27 January, 2019; Gemäldegalerie, Berlin, 1 March–30 June, 2019), London, 2018, pp. 164–65; C. R. Puglisi and W. L. Barcham, *Art and Faith in the Venetian Art World*, Turnhout 2019, pp. 164–65; P. Humfrey, *Giovanni Bellini*, Venice, 2021, pp. 106–7; G. Zavatta, "Giovanni Bellini's Pietà di Rimini: exhibitions and restorations (1930-2019)", *Storia dell'Arte*, 158 no. 2, 2022, pp. 26–47; and G. A. Calogero, *Giovanni Bellini. La lentezza del genio*, Cinisello Balsamo, 2025, pp. 125–26. New information about the transfer of the painting from the Tempio Malatestiano to the Palazzo Comunale in the early nineteenth century is provided by the essay by Giulio Zavatta in the present publication.

2 A. Campana, "Notizie sulla *Pietà* riminese di Giovanni Bellini," in *Scritti di Storia dell'arte in onore di Marco Salmi*, ed. by V. Martinelli and F.M. Aliberti, Rome, 1962, II, pp. 405–27.

3 Campana, 1962, p. 411; A. Giovanardi, "La *docta religio* di un dipinto. Erudizione e devozione nella *Pietà* riminese di Giovanni Bellini," in *Gli angeli della Pietà. Intorno a Giovanni Bellini*, exhibition catalog (Museo della Città, Rimini, 19 August–4 November, 2012), ed. by M. Bona Castellotto and M. Pulini, Turin, 2012, p. 17.

4 G. Vasari, *Le Vite de' più eccellenti Architetti, Pittori er Scultori Italiani* (1550), ed. by L. Bellosi and A. Rossi, Turin, 1986, p. 437; G. Vasari, *Le Vite de' più eccellenti Pittori, Scultori e Architettori* (1568), ed. by P. Della Pergola *et al.*, Novara, 1967, vol. III, p. 97.

5 R. Adimari, *Sito Riminese*, Brescia, 1616, vol. I, p. 66; C. F. Marcheselli, *Pitture della Chiese di Rimini*, Rimini, 1754, p. 31.

6 Campana, 1962, pp. 419, 426.

7 For this work, see Lucco, 2019, pp. 365–67, with arguments for the reliability of the recorded inscription with the date.

8 As suggested by A. Giovanardi, "La luce sepolta. Appunti sulla *Pietà* riminese di Giovanni Bellini," *Parola e Tempo*, no. XI, 2012, p. 346.

9 For a recent survey of these paintings as a group, see Puglisi and Barcham, 2019, pp. 154–176.

10 See Peta Motture in *Carvings, Casts and Collectors. The Art of Renaissance Sculpture*, ed. by P. Motture, E. Jones and D. Zikos, London, 2013, pp. 21–31.

11 The recent book by Calogero, 2025, differs sharply from the accounts of the early career before about 1470 by Lucco, 2019, and by myself (Humfrey, 2021). However, the author (p. 126) agrees with my own dating, by now conventional, of the Rimini *Pietà* to circa 1470 (p. 126)—that is to say, close to the lost *Saint Catherine of Siena* altarpiece, and mid-way between the *Saint Vincent Ferrer* polyptych and the Pesaro *Coronation of the Virgin*.

12 For an analysis of the technique of the London painting, see J. Dunkerton and M. Spring, "Giovanni Bellini's Painting Technique," *National Gallery Technical Bulletin*, no. XXXIX, 2018, pp. 44–49.

13 See the detailed discussion by Lucco, 2019, pp. 370–74. In my opinion, the author's dating to circa 1472–75—very close, in other words, to the Rimini *Pietà*—is somewhat too late. By contrast, I find the dating by Calogero (p. 54) of the Brera painting to circa 1460 much too early.

14 Campana, 1962. See also Giovanardi, "La docta religio," 2012; Giovanardi, "La luce sepolta," 2012, pp. 345–46.

15 Campana, 1962, p. 427.

16 Ibid., p. 421.

17 E. Battisti, *Piero della Francesca*, revised edition, Milan, 1992, pp. 323–25, 413 note 582, 622.

18 Humfrey, 2021, pp. 70–72.

19 J. A. Crowe and G. B. Cavalcaselle, *History of Painting in North Italy*, London, 1871, vol. I, p. 601. The authors did not identify it with the work described by Vasari, which they listed as lost (p. 194).

20 R. Longhi, "Piero dei Franceschi e lo sviluppo della pittura veneziana," *L'Arte*, no. XVII, 1914, p. 244 note 1.

21 P. Paoletti, *La Scuola Grande di San Marco*, Venice, 1929, p. 147 note 1.

22 C. Gamba, *Giovanni Bellini*, Milan, 1937, pp. 69–70.

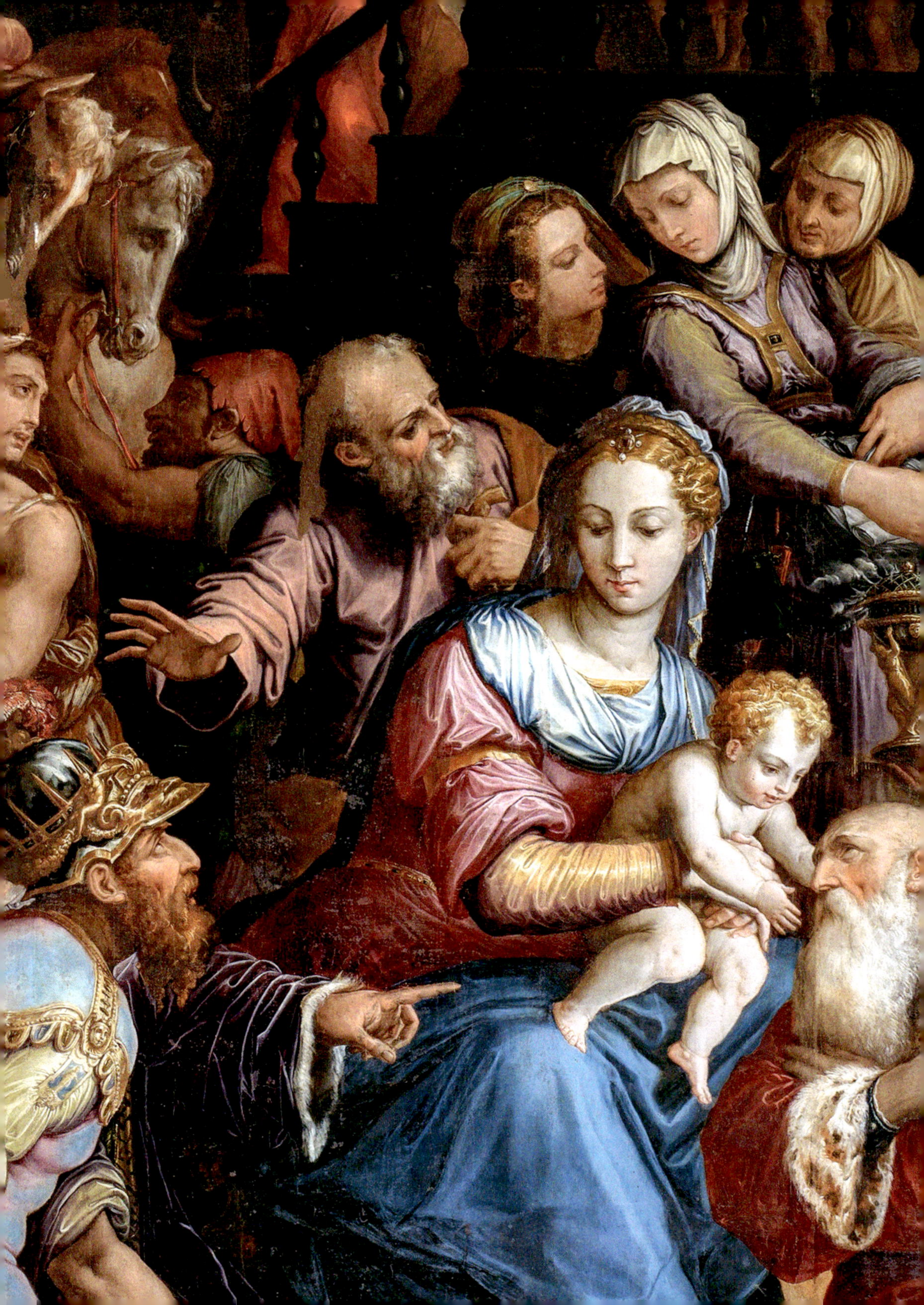

The Shadow of Sigismondo: Vasari and Bellini's *Pietà* in Rimini, a Chronicle of a Difficult Relationship

Giovanni Sassu

"Something different and more."

Almost fifty years ago, Giovanni Previtali, with one of his habitual catch-phrases, summarized the relation between Andrea Mantegna and Giovanni Bellini noting how the two celebrated painters, notwithstanding their similar cultural backgrounds (Padua, Venice, knowledge of the works of Donatello and Piero) and the points of contact between their artistic careers, ended up taking different paths, with Mantegna taking on the role of the humanist and Bellini becoming "something different and more."[1]

The *Pietà (Dead Christ supported by Four Angels)* in Rimini is perhaps one of the most emblematic examples of this "divergent affinity," which now has the possibility of being further explored thanks to the novel information emerging from the restoration of this masterpiece.

An extraordinary work, capable of transforming the "sublimation of pain into an almost silent elegy,"[2] Bellini's *Pietà* in Rimini is also, in many ways, a nebula fraught with unanswered questions, from its placement in the chronology of the great painter's career to the identity of the patron, to its true original location.

The purpose of the present paper is to review the data already available to us. Not in the hope of any miraculous discoveries, but rather to sort the certain from the uncertain, the probable from the possible, and to re-examine information that has often been taken too much for granted.

February 1499

Among the oldest documents found so far, there are two that explicitly mention Bellini's work in Rimini, both associated with Rainerio di Lodovico Migliorati, a courtier of the Malatesta family. The first document is Migliorati's will, drawn up in his home in the district of Santa Maria in Trivio on February 17, 1499; the second is the inventory of his property, drawn up in the same month, perhaps after Migliorati's death. Both documents were published and masterfully commented by Augusto Campana in 1962.[3] In both, we find mention of a *Pietà* that can be unquestionably identified as the work located in the Museo della Città di Rimini "Luigi Tonini".

In the will, the work is described as "unam ipsius testatoris tabulam depictam manu Iohannis Bellini, in qua est depicta imago domini nostri Iesu Christi Salvatoris mortui et sublati de cruce in formam pietatis" (one of the testator's own paintings, painted by the hand of Giovanni Bellini, in which is depicted the image of our Lord Jesus Christ the Savior, dead and taken down from the cross in the form of piety). While in the inventory it is described as "an altarpiece or panel depicting the image of Our Lord Jesus Christ in the form of Pietà, descended from the cross."[4]

We now have a little more information on Rainerio Migliorati than what was available to Campana. We know that he held several positions in Rimini under the Malatesta, mainly of an administrative and political nature: *vicario delle gabelle* (a tax collector), advisor to Sigismondo and Pandolfo Malatesta (for the latter he also served as spokesman to the pope), and even supervisor of the construction work on the palace of their mother, Elisabetta Aldobrandini.[5]

We know he was also involved in the leading cultural circles of the time, as the number of works listed in his inventory suggests. Not a true collector, of course, but certainly a lover of antiquities who bought items and traded them with his friends. He was also a lover of books, and had assembled a great library which he left to the Franciscans.[6] Among his acquaintances were great humanists like Roberto Valturio and Roberto Orsi, who paid homage to him in Latin verse,[7] and he was in contact with artists like Marco di Giovanni, who worked for him as a miniaturist. We also have documents attesting that Piero della Francesca was staying at Migliorati's home in Rimini when he signed a mysterious annual lease for a small apartment in the San Simone district on April 22, 1482, with the painter Gabriele di Stefano as witness.[8] This then was the man who owned Giovanni Bellini's *Pietà*. Let us return, however, to the two documents, referring readers to the known works for the full texts.

Migliorati's familiarity with the Malatesta family is well known, but not enough emphasis has been placed on his absolute trust in Violante Bentivoglio, the lady who had married Pandolfo IV in 1485.[9] In his testament Migliorati names her as trustee and executor. The document specifies that this young woman—whose gentle and delicate features we know from the family portrait that appears in Ghirlandaio's altarpiece in San Cataldo[10]—was entrusted with taking care of the dying man's material affairs, but above all with fulfilling his wish: the construction of a family chapel in the prestigious church of Sant'Antonio Abate, a church that is no longer extant but was adjacent to church of San Francesco, that is, the Tempio Malatestiano.[11] Finally, at the end of the will, we find the indication that the chapel is to house Bellini's panel, described with the Latin words quoted above.[12]

There is little doubt that the will attests to the dying man's firm intention of having built something that did not yet exist. The location of the chapel within the church is specified (where the image of the Virgin Mary and Saint James is painted), as are the resources necessary to build it and even the grandiose dimensions of the monument, destined to house the remains of Rainerio and of those deceased members of his family buried in the church of San Francesco.[13] No plans are attached, but there is no doubt that Migliorati had a clear idea of what he wanted, to the point of specifying that the chapel had to be based on those recently built in the church of Santa Maria dei Servi and in the church of San Giovanni Evangelista in Rimini. The latter are not casual examples, but specific courtly models and typical Malatesta monuments. The one in San Giovanni Evangelista most likely corresponds to the chapel that, according to Fantaguzzi's chronicle, Pandolfo Malatesta had ordered in 1498 as a votive offering after the foiling of the Adimari conspiracy.[14] It is quite evident that even in his final decisions, Migliorati continued to act as courtier, following the artistic choices of the ruling family.

As noted above, the *Pietà* is mentioned also in the inventory written a few days after the will. Here too, there is no doubt about the identity of the work. While its description as an "ancona o vero taula" (altarpiece or panel) may certainly raise eyebrows, it does correctly suggest the devotional value that the work had for its owner, who, most likely kept it above an altar and prayed to it.

Vasari as false witness?

So far, so good.

And yet, notwithstanding the clearly stated directions in the will, it seems to me most likely that the Migliorati chapel was never built. This is suggested by two elements of proof that while not decisive are most substantial. The first is that in the list of tombs in the church of Sant'Antonio Abate recorded by Friar Francesco Antonio Righini, there is no mention of Migliorati, his remains, or his chapel.[15] The second is that fifty-one years later, the presence of an "image of Our Lord Jesus Christ in the form of piety" is attested instead in the church of San Francesco, witnessed by none other than Giorgio Vasari.

This is where things get complicated for Bellini scholars: when consulting the biography of the great Venetian painter in the *Vite*, the account varies slightly between the two editions.[16] In the 1550 Torrentino version (fig. 1), we find the following:

> Nor will I talk any more of the works he sent around the dominion of Venice and the many portraits of princes that he made, without counting all the parts of large paintings he made for them, such as in Rimini for Signor Sigismondo Malatesta, a painting of a Pietà held up by two cherubs, which is now in San Francesco in that city.

In the Giunti edition (fig. 2), published in 1568, the passage takes on a slightly different character:

> But to return to the works of Giovanni, that is, to his principal works, for it would take too long to try to make mention of all the pictures and

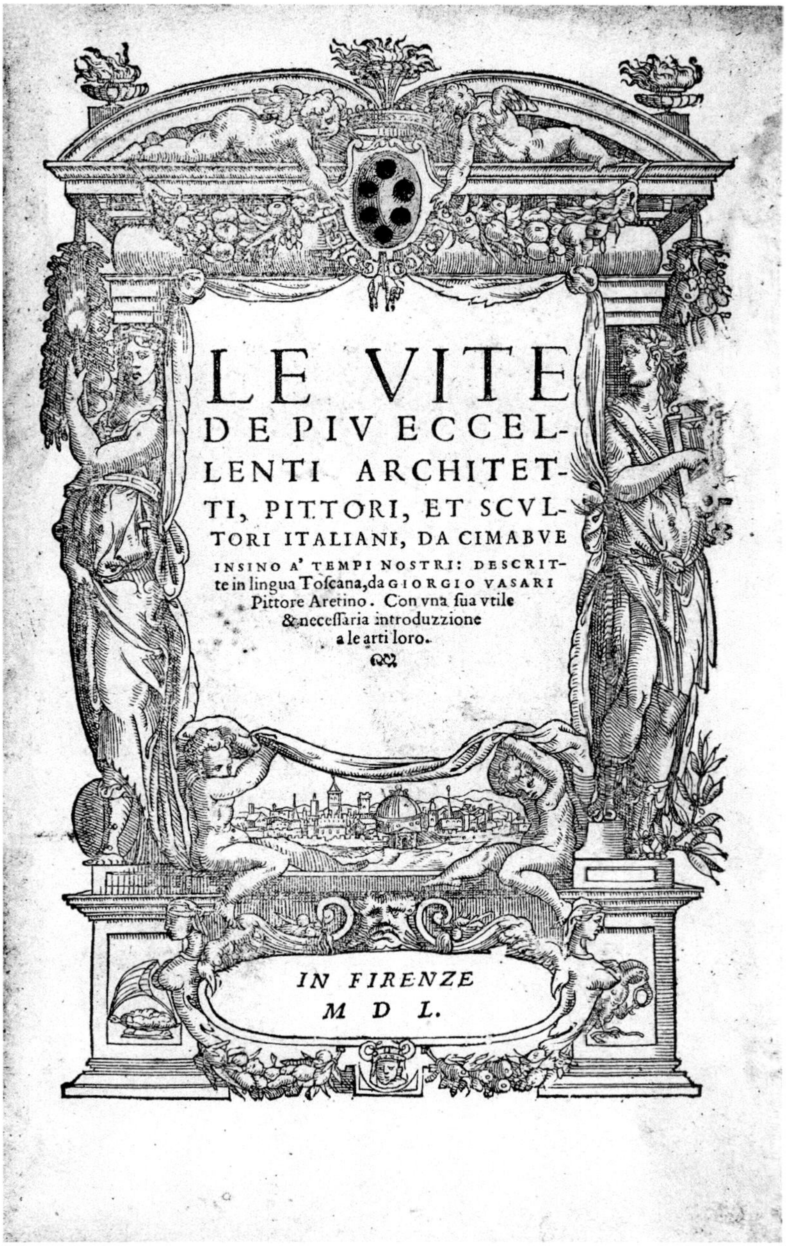

LE VITE
DE PIV ECCEL-
LENTI ARCHITET-
TI, PITTORI, ET SCVL-
TORI ITALIANI, DA CIMABVE
INSINO A' TEMPI NOSTRI: DESCRIT-
te in lingua Toscana, da GIORGIO VASARI
Pittore Aretino. Con vna sua vtile
& necessaria introduzzione
a le arti loro.

IN FIRENZE
M D L.

1
Title page of the first edition of Vasari's *Vite*, Florence, L. Torrentino, 1550

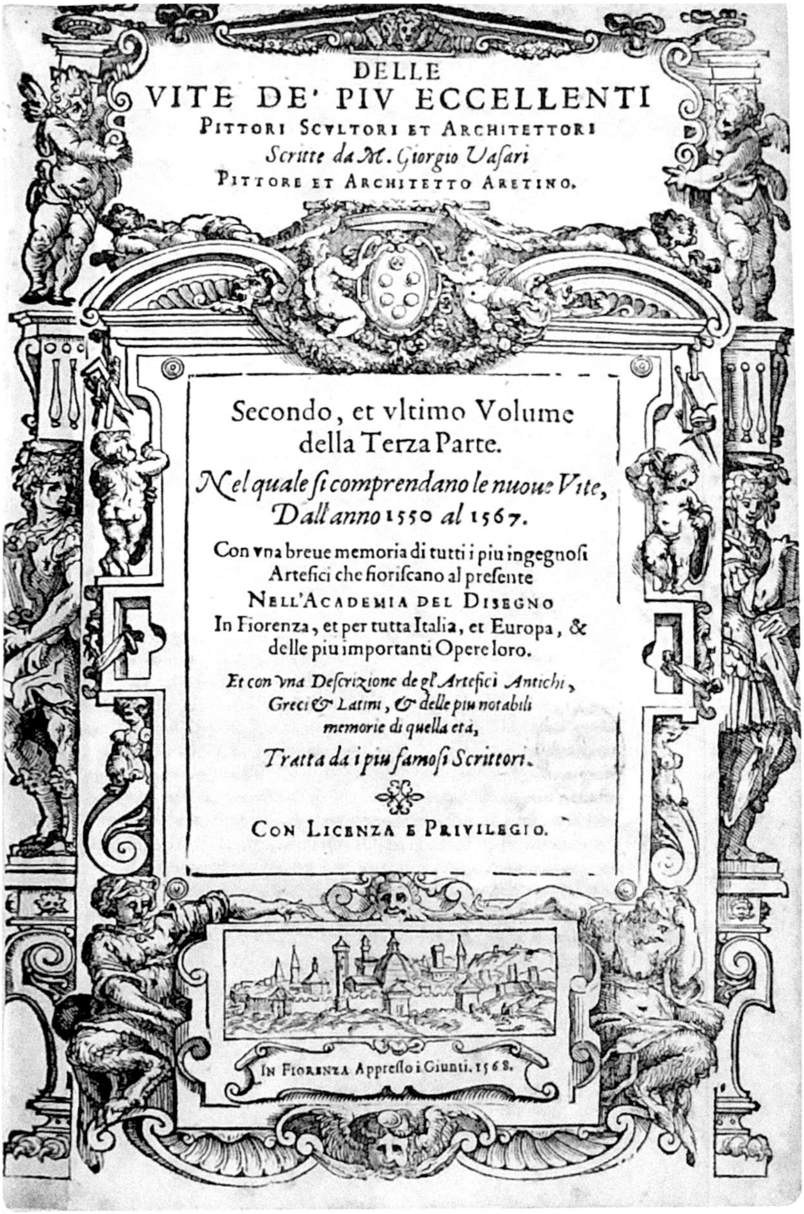

DELLE
VITE DE' PIV ECCELLENTI
PITTORI SCVLTORI ET ARCHITETTORI
Scritte da M. Giorgio Vaſari
PITTORE ET ARCHITETTO ARETINO.

Secondo, et vltimo Volume
della Terza Parte.
Nel quale ſi comprendano le nuoue Vite,
Dall'anno 1550 al 1567.
Con vna breue memoria di tutti i piu ingegnoſi
Artefici che fioriſcano al preſente
NELL'ACADEMIA DEL DISEGNO
In Fiorenza, et per tutta Italia, et Europa, &
delle piu importanti Opere loro.
Et con vna Deſcrizione de gl'Artefici Antichi,
Greci & Latini, & delle piu notabili
memorie di quella età,
Tratta da i piu famoſi Scrittori.

CON LICENZA E PRIVILEGIO.

IN FIORENZA Appreſſo i Giunti. 1568.

2
Title page of the second edition
of Vasari's *Vite*, Florence, Giunti, 1568

> portraits that are in the houses of gentlemen in Venice and in other parts of that country. In Rimini, for Signor Sigismondo Malatesta, he made a large picture containing a Pieta, supported by two little boys, which is now in S. Francesco in that city.

These are two very well-known passages that generations of scholars have grappled with and variously interpreted.[17]

In this context, it may be useful to try to outline the differences between the two versions. Regarding the location and destination of the *Pietà*, in the Torrentino edition the emphasis is on who commissioned it (Sigismondo) and where the work is currently located. In the Giunti version, the information is repeated, but with the specification that it was "a large painting." The context is also interesting: in the Torrentiniana, the work is cited as one example among many of works sent to various places, along with "many portraits of princes" and the "other various things like some large paintings" he made for them. The *Pietà* is presented as one of Bellini's many works distributed throughout the Venetian domains. In the Giunti, the work is described as one of the Venetian artist's "major" works ("to return to the works of Giovanni, that is, to the major ones..."), immediately after the reference to Ariosto's mention of Bellini as one of the best painters of his time.

Bellini specialists have always noted at least three problems in identifying Vasari's *Pietà* with the one at hand. The first is Vasari's statement that the patron was Sigismondo Malatesta. Scholars tend to rule this out because the work is considered stylistically posterior—for some around 1470, for most around 1474—to the death of the prince (October 1468). The second problem is his reference to a "large painting," whereas the panel has a base of only 132 cm. Finally, and most decisively, the number of angels supporting Christ in our *Pietà* is four, not two.

To address these issues, it is important to take into account the context in which the Rimini entries in the *Vite* were written, an aspect that has been often underestimated. It has always seemed plausible that Vasari was familiar with the Tempio Malatestiano, given that he painted the large canvas *Saint Francis receiving the stigmata* for the high altar, commissioned by Carlo Marcheselli. The work was painted over a very short period: on January 4,

1548, Vasari received the commission through an intermediary; he painted it at the client's home and completed it by the end of the following February.[18]

He was already in Rimini because Abbot Giovan Matteo Faetani of Santa Maria di Scolca had offered him his services and those of "one of his monks, an [exc]ellent writer" ("un suo monaco, ecc[ellente] scrittore") to assemble and transcribe the manuscript of the *Vite* to be printed by Lorenzo Torrentino.[19] Vasari's *Ricordanze*, and his correspondence convey his frenetic activity at this important juncture in his life and are clear about his movements. From October 1547, the artist was at the Olivetan monastery, on the hill of Covignano, working on the wonderful *Adoration of the Magi* (fig. 3) and the decoration of the chapel, which he completed at the end of 1547. He then set to work—as mentioned above, between January and February 1548—on the Franciscan altarpiece and on the *Deposition* of Ravenna, finally returning to Arezzo in early March, if not earlier.[20]

It seems likely, perhaps even obvious, that Vasari must have had the opportunity to examine the *Pietà de visu*. Also because the commission for the altar piece in San Francesco was accompanied by the promise of working in the home of Marcheselli (now known as Palazzo Lettimi), located a few meters from the church. Yet, a margin of uncertainty remains in regards to Vasari's actual visits to the place or, at least, to the accuracy of his observations. The doubt arises from the specific location of the *Pietà*. We know that, about fifty years after Vasari's last mentioned it, the work was in the Sacristy, a room "very well furnished with various vestments and of great value," as Raffaele Adimari reported in 1616.[21] This room is identified with the current Cella delle Reliquie, and it is on the counter-façade of this chapel that, in 1451, Piero della Francesca had painted the icon par excellence of the Malatesta period: the fresco of *Sigismondo Pandolfo Malatesta in prayer before Saint Sigismund*.[22] Yet, there is no mention of this fresco or of a visit to Rimini by Piero in the *Vite*: can one really imagine Vasari seeing Bellini's *Pietà* and failing to note the presence of the great fresco by an artist he admired, and in which, moreover, the "patron" of the *Pietà* itself was depicted? How is, furthermore, that, given that among the works in the church of San Francesco mentioned in the Torrentino edition we find only those by Giotto (in a famous, long, and confused passage in which Vasari does not mention

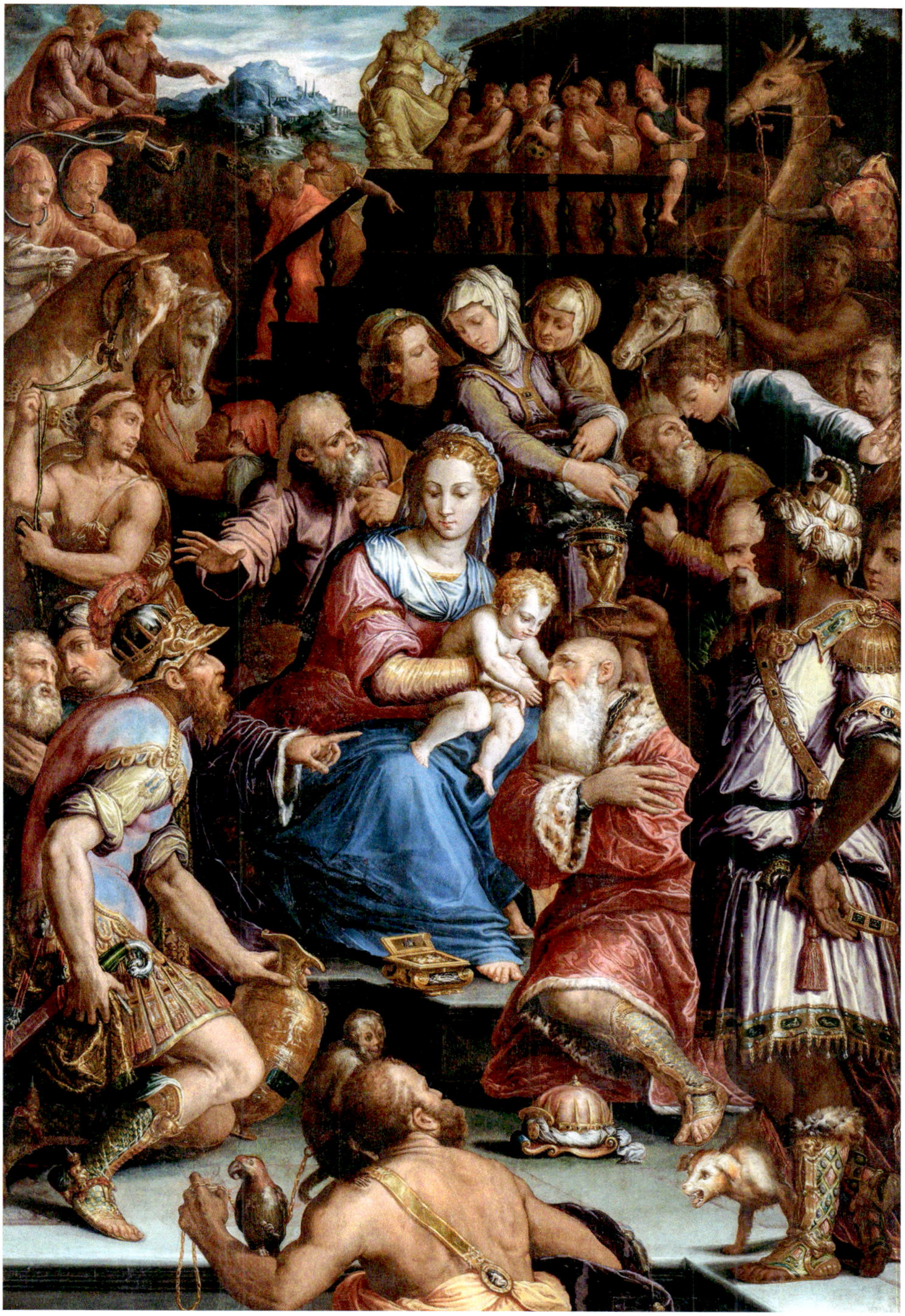

3
Giorgio Vasari, *Adoration of the Magi*, 1547, panel, 340 × 250 cm, Rimini, San Fortunato (Abbey of Santa Maria di Scolca)

the *Crucifix*)? And why, in the Vasari's first version of the biography of the much-admired Leon Battista Alberti, is the church of San Francesco dismissed in barely two lines.[23] In the Giunti edition of the *Vite* we do find a more comprehensive description of San Francesco and of the works it contained by Alberti, as well as those by Matteo de' Pasti, Agostino di Duccio, and others.[24] But, even here, what is the quality of the eyewitness account? We know that Vasari returned to Rimini between April 20 and 24, 1566, during a journey that took him from Ancona to Bologna via Ravenna. However, as he himself told Vincenzo Borghini, he was on a very tight schedule, which suggests that his information on "Arimino" may have derived from a very hasty personal survey or from second-hand sources.[25]

If one considers all of the above, also in light of the general critical reassessment that Vasari carried out between the first and second edition of the *Vite*, one is left with the impression that the information on the *Pietà* in the first edition was somewhat of a last-minute addition. The more so considering that the Rimini fair copy of the *Vite* was already assembled in December 1447 and that Vasari began working in San Francesco only around the following January.[26] In the Giunti edition, as we have seen, Bellini's work is described as one of his great works. As for the author's description of it as a "large" painting, it is possible that in rereading the passage from 1550, Vasari was misled by his own earlier mention of larger paintings.

Even on the number of the cherubs ("Pietà with two cherubs holding it"), we need to be more understanding with Vasari. At least in the Torrentiniana edition, Vasari's visual descriptions were not always the most accurate. When he speaks of the *Pietà* it is clear that under this label he is including compositional formulas ranging from the dead Christ in the Virgin's lap to the dead Christ surrounded by a group of faithful, along with *the Imago pietatis* proper, that is, Jesus supported by angels or other holy figures.

In the descriptions of the latter subjects, Vasari is at times quite precise, as in the case of Perugino's *Lamentation over the Dead Christ*, now in the Uffizi, where he correctly describes the four figures in the background. More often, however, his descriptions are generic and sometimes even inaccurate. Among his generic descriptions are the *Pietàs* without further specification, a term he employs—as we do today—for well-defined iconographic types (such as the *Vesperbild*, exemplified by Michelangelo's *Pietà* in St. Peter's). In most cases, however, he mentions the presence of Mary and is at times very precise (as in the case of Sebastiano del Piombo's *Pietà* in Madrid), and at times he neglects important aspects, as in the case Perin del Vaga's *Lamentation of Christ* in Santo Stefano al Cacco in Rome. In the latter, Vasari describes a "Pietà with the dead Christ in the lap of Our Lady" and names the patron, but fails to mention the three figures looking down at Jesus: the Evangelist, Mary Magdalene, and Nicodemus.[27]

In short, in the light of Vasari's working method which required collecting scattered information and processing it at a later stage, sometimes years later, it is advisable to always take with one or two grains of salt the information reported in the *Vite*, especially when it comes to descriptive details.

To conclude our discussion of Vasari, it has often been repeated—aside from the doubts on the chronology of the work and as Campana had already suggested—that Vasari's attribution of the commission to Sigismondo must be seen as the probable result of a misleading local testimony, made plausible by the fame of the supposed patron and the location of the painting inside a church filled with his emblems. In the light of these doubts, attempts have also been made to look elsewhere in the family, suggesting the implausible name of Carlo (born too late, on October 23, 1480), or that of his father Roberto. But even in the latter case, the period during which the famous Magnifico developed relations with Venice—relations that would have made it possible to commission the work to the Venetian painter—does not correspond to the dating of our work.[28]

What then?

What then? After reviewing this long parade of doubts, it is worth trying to summarize what we do know.

1: it is highly implausible that two *Pietàs* by Bellini coexisted within a few square meters: Vasari could not have failed to discover and mention such an amazing coincidence, and the same holds for our other sources on Rimini.

2: we must accept the possibility that Vasari either misinterpreted or misdescribed the painting. Whether his description was based on his own recollection or that of one of his sources, such as Faetani for example, is here irrelevant.[29]

3: there is no trace of Rainerio Migliorati's tomb in the document listing the funeral monuments in Sant'Antonio Abate in the eighteenth century.[30]

The change of location from the one indicated by Migliorati to one that later became historical has actually a simple explanation: Violante Bentivoglio in Malatesta did not carry out the wishes of her husband's faithful advisor, due the difficult political situation that developed after Migliorati's death. Only, a few months after the will was drawn up, things took a turn for the worse for Pandolfo Malatesta. The pope obtained the green light from France and Spain for his son Cesare Borgia's ambitions in the province of Romagna, and on August 16, 1499, a first step was taken in a process that that led to Pandolfaccio being stripped of his title as vicar of Rimini. The following year, Cesare Borgia led his army to the gates of Rimini. On October 10, 1500, the city surrendered, while Pandolfo, having already shipped his family to safety, took refuge in the city fortress where he resisted for a few days before agreeing to leave the city to its new master.[31]

It was in this confused and dramatic situation that the painting must have been first acquired by the Malatesta family (and possibly the apocryphal signature added) and then placed among the family's possessions in the church of San Francesco, followed by the decision to ignore the owner's final wish.

Migliorati, in the light of the unreliability of Vasari's testimony, must necessarily be confirmed as the true owner of the work. As we have seen, this figure deserves to be individually studied: he is one of the typical protagonists of the Malatesta era, and his death in 1499 seems indeed to herald the decline and fall of the family. As for his relations with Venice, we have unfortunately no more than what Campana had already discovered: a trip made on behalf of Pandolfo at the end of November 1496. Too little to speculate about a possible long-distance commission or a direct purchase in Venice, but also too little not to investigate any further.[32]

It is also for this reason, as well as to dispel the shadow of Sigismondo once and for all, that the restoration appears as a crucial step towards a more adequate understanding of our *Pietà*, along with a source of reliable information on the working technique, and in particular the use or not of oil painting (which, however, even if confirmed would not necessarily date the work to the years of Bellini's exchanges with Antonello da Messina).[33]

And here, in short, the problem of the dating returns. On this, I will leave the floor to those who know Bellini well, namely Peter Humfrey in the present volume. Allow me only to add that I have never been convinced by Longhi's parallel with the *Pesaro Altarpiece*: the *Pietà* of Rimini appears to me to be rather a sophisticated product of Bellini's Mantegna phase and very distant from the soft contours of the painting in Pesaro.[34]

In conclusion, the dispute over the chronology of the Bellini's masterpiece remains alive and is even more compelling. Destabilizing certainties is the fate of the great icons of art history.

In writing these pages, I have been fortunate to benefit from the help of Nadia Bizzocchi, Giacomo Alberto Calogero, Luca Giorgini, Peter Humfrey, Mauro Lucco, Marco Musmeci, Lucia Tori, Giovanni Carlo Federico Villa, and, in particular, Giulio Zavatta.

My gratitude extends to Venetian Heritage, Toto Bergamo Rossi, and his magnificent team, who made possible a project that I, as Director of the Museums of Rimini, had hoped for from the first to the last day of my term between 2022 and 2024.

1 G. Previtali, *La periodizzazione della storia dell'arte italiana*, in *Storia dell'arte italiana*, vol. I: *Questioni e metodi*, Turin 1979, p. 49.

2 M. Lucco, *Giovanni Bellini. Catalogo ragionato,* Ponzano Veneto, 2020, p. 375; please refer to this extensive entry for the bibliography on the work prior to 2020: pp. 375–77 cat. 45. To be supplemented now by the one cited by P. Humfrey in the present volume and by C.A. Calogero, *Giovanni Bellini. La lentezza del genio,* Cinisello Balsamo 2025, p. 126.

3 A. Campana, *Notizie sulla* Pietà *riminese di Giovanni Bellini,* in *Scritti di Storia dell'arte in onore di Mario Salmi,* ed. by V. Martinelli, F.M. Aliberti, vol. II, Rome, 1962, pp. 405–27 (after a brief but incomplete citation of the same document by L. Tonini, *Storia civile e sacra riminese,* Rimini ,1882, vol. V, p. 601). Now in O. Delucca, *Artisti a Rimini fra gotico e Rinascimento,* preface by P.G. Pasini, Rimini, 1997, pp. 535, 691. The two documents are in the Archivio di Stato di Rimini, A. Mangiaroli, 1499; ff. 63–70 (Migliorati's will), 218–229 (inventory).

4 Campana, 1962, pp. 418–19, 426. For an insightful interpretation of the term "sublati," see A. Marchi in *Il Tempio Malatestiano a Rimini*, ed. by A. Paolucci, Modena 2010, vol. I, p. 253.

5 On Migliorati, among others see: Tonini, 1882, pp. 398, 601; C. Grigioni, "Un soggiorno ignorato di Piero della Francesca in Rimini," *Rassegna*

bibliografica dell'Arte Italiana, no. XII, 7–9, 1909, p. 119; Campana, 1862, pp. 417–27; Delucca, 1997, pp. 118 (on his role as a courtier), 391–92 (on his supervising of the construction of the Aldobrandini building); R. Copioli, *Gli Agolanti e il castello di Riccione,* Rimini, 2003, p. 93 (kinship with the Malatesta family).

6 On the Franciscan library and the Migliorati bequest: see G. Mazzantini, "La Biblioteca di San Francesco (Tempio Malatestiano) in Rimini," in *Scritti vari di filologia,* Rome, 1901, pp. 345–52, in particular p. 346.

7 See also Campana, 1862, pp. 425–27.

8 Grigioni, 1909, pp. 118–21.

9 On her personality and the Pandolfo period, see G.L. Masetti Zannini and A. Falcioni (eds.), *La signoria di Pandolfo IV Malatesti (1482–1528),* Rimini, 2003.

10 G. Milantoni, in *Pittura a Rimini tra gotico e manierismo,* exhibition catalog (Sala delle Colonne, Rimini, August–September 1979), Rimini 1979, pp. 48–52.

11 The church, destroyed in 1758, was located close to the apse of the church of San Francesco. The most important information is still that provided by C. Ricci, *Il Tempio malatestiano,* first edition Milan–Rome 1924; reprinted with an appendix by P. G. Pasini, Rimini 1974, pp. 180-186.

12 Campana, *Notizie* cit., pp. 417-419; Delucca, 1997, pp. 535, 691.

13 Campana, 1862, pp. 421–22. There has been and continues to be a great deal of controversy on this point: D. Benati, in *Pittura a Rimini,* 1979, pp. 40–41, writes that the bequest was linked to the Malatestian Temple; M. Pulini, in *Gli angeli della* Pietà. *Intorno a Giovanni Bellini,* exhibition catalog (Museo della Città, Rimini, August 19–November 4, 2012), ed. by M. Bona Castellotti and M. Pulini, Turin, 2012, p. 7, argues that the documents place it in Sant'Antonio Abate. As we have seen, the documents testify otherwise. Based on available information, Alessandro Parronchi calculated a width of 9.30 meters for the Migliorati tomb, also attempting to draw its shape: Letter from A. Parronchi to A. Campana, February 13, 1961, Rimini, Biblioteca Gambalunga, Archivio Campana, drawer 4, file Bellini. I am grateful to my friend Zavatta for bringing these documents to my attention. It is my own fault that I did not make full use of the information they contain.

14 Campana, 1862, p. 423, dates these three chapels to the second golden age of Rimini architecture, between the end of the fifteenth and the beginning of the sixteenth century, along with the façade of Santa Maria di Scolca, the construction of Santa Maria della Colonnella, the Tempietto di Sant'Antonio, the Ricciardelli and Marcheselli-Lettimi palaces, and the so-called Casa di Isotta, no longer extant.

15 Among the countless pieces of information collected by F. A. Righini, *Nuovo ed esatto campione di questo nostro convento de min[ori]: con[ventua]li di s. Francesco di questa città di Rimino,* 1756, Forlì, Biblioteca Comunale, Piancastelli Collection, ms. 0,1/3, there is also a list of tombs in Sant'Antonio Abate (see reproduction in Ricci, 1924, p. 185, fig. 240). Campana had already mentioned this (1862, p. 423).

16 I am quoting from G. Vasari, *Le Vite de' più eccellenti architetti, pittori, et scultori italiani, da Cimabue insino a' tempi nostri,* Florence, 1550; ed. by L. Bellosi and A. Rossi, introduction by G. Previtali, Turin, 1986, p. 437; and from G. Vasari, *Le Vite de' più eccellenti pittori, scultori e architettori,* Florence, 1568, ed. by P. Della Pergola, L. Grassi, G. Previtali, Novara 1967, vol. III, p. 97.

17 Campana, 1862, pp. 413–16, discusses the two versions. For the import of Vasari's words for scholars of Bellini, see the summary in Lucco, 2020, pp. 375–77 cat. 45.

18 See: G. Vasari, *Libro delle Ricordanze,* Archivio Vasari, no. 31, f. 17*v* (commission of January 4, mediated by Giovan Matteo Faetani, whom we will discuss shortly; the name of the client is poorly annotated); K. Frey, *Der literarische Nachlass Giorgio Vasaris,* Munich 1930, vol. II, pp. 216–17 (in February the work is in progress); G. Vasari, *Descrizione delle opere di Giorgio Vasari,* in *Le Vite* (1568), vol. VIII, p. 240 (for the description of the work). Many of the documents cited here are transcribed in https://vasariscrittore.memofonte.it/archivio.
On the Marcheselli altarpiece and the Rimini studies, see P. G. Pasini, "Il quadro del Vasari nel Duomo di Rimini," *Rivista Diocesana di Rimini,* no. 33, 1968, pp. 63–64, and G. Zavatta, Giorgio Vasari e Nicolas Cordier a Rimini: due disegni dal "Salon du Dessin" di Parigi, e una novità da Edimburgo, *L'Arco,* nos. 1–2, 2007, pp. 40–47, with previous bibliography.

19 The events surrounding the publication in M.S. Campanini, "Faitani, Giovan Matteo," in *Dizionario Biografico degli Italiani,* vol. 44, 1994; see also: https://www.treccani.it/enciclopedia/giovan-matteo-faitani_(Dizionario-Biografico)/.

20 The commission for Scolca dates back to August 9, 1547. Vasari sent Benedetto Spadari ahead to prepare the panel, but he only reached Rimini at the beginning of October. By December, the altar had been completed and work was underway on the frescoes in the chapel (see

Vasari, *Libro delle Ricordanze*, f. 17*r*, for the timing of the work; the letter addressed to him in Romagna by L. Domenichi: Frey, 1930, pp. 202–05 for his presence in Rimini from October). A different chronology about the return to Arezzo can be found in B. Agosti, *Giorgio Vasari. Luoghi e tempi delle Vite*, Milan 2025, pp. 81–82.

21 R. Adimari, *Sito riminese,* Brescia, 1616, vol. I, p. 68 ("And in the sacristy there is still a beautiful painting of a Pietà by Giovanni Bellino, a very famous painter of his time, which is considered to be of the highest quality and great value"). For the identification of the sacristy with the reliquary, see M. Campigli in *Il Tempio Malatestiano*, 2010, p. 243. The *Pietà* is also seen in the sacristy in the eighteenth century, see at least: C. F. Marcheselli, *Pitture delle Chiese di Rimini,* Rimini, 1754, p. 31 ("it was made in Venice by order of Sigismondo Malatesta"); and G. B. Costa, "Il Tempio di S. Francesco di Rimino," in *Miscellanei di varia letteratura*, Lucca, 1765, vol. V, p. 118.

22 On the fresco, since 2001, in the Chapel of the Conception after its removal in 1943, see as a starting point P. G. Pasini, *Il Tempio malatestiano. Splendore cortese e classicismo umanistico,* Geneva–Milan, 2000, pp. 34–36; A. Paolucci in *Il Tempio*, 2010, pp. 220–24.

23 The long passage on Giotto with the "many paintings" in the church destroyed by "Gismondo," the frescoes in the cloister, including the stories of the blessed Michelina (not his due to obvious chronological limitations of the person depicted) and a Saint Thomas Aquinas: Vasari, *Le Vite* (1550), pp. 123–25; the scant passage on Alberti: ibid., pp. 356–57.

24 See Vasari, *Le Vite (*1568), *ad indicem.*

25 Frey, 1930, pp. 234, 235 ("From our party in Loreto and Ancona, who wrote them, I have been to Rimini and Ravenna, where I saw the things you desired and measured the Ritonda, and there is much to discuss, and many things are being done for her").

26 In *Descrizione...*, 1568, pp. 239–40, Vasari recalls the services of the Olivetans of Rimini on the manuscript of *Le Vite.* In December 1547, the Olivetan version of the text must have already been ready, as evidenced by the feedback on the first draft received in December by Paolo Giovio and Annibal Caro: cf. Frey, 1930, pp. 209–13 (on January 29, Giovio sent a detailed account of what he had read, cf. ibid., pp. 215–16). See A. Rossi, *Nota testologica* in Vasari, *Le Vite* (1568), pp. XXXI–XXXII. The "Olivetan" manuscript has been lost, but a page was found by P. Scapecchi, "Una carta dell'esemplare riminese delle Vite del Vasari con correzioni di Giambullari. Nuove indicazioni e proposte per la torrentiniana," *Mitteilungen des Kunsthistorischen Institutes in Florenz*, vol. 42, no. 1, 1998, pp. 101–14.

27 For all the descriptions cited, see Vasari, *Le Vite* (1550), pp. 713, 844, 856, 885.

28 Carlo Malatesta is mentioned by Paoletti, 1929, p. 147 note 1. The Roberto hypothesis is cautiously put forward by Marchi in *Il Tempio malatestiano*, 2010, p. 254, who also hypothesizes that "the Magnifico" sealed a negotiation begun by his father.

29 According to Campanini, Faitani (1994) may have served as correspondent and source also beyond Rimini.

30 The tomb of Elisabetta degli Atti, commissioned in 1488, is also not listed, but it is not known whether it was ever built: see M. Bona Castellotti, *Il Re della gloria,* in *Gli angeli*, 2012, p. 13.

31 A. Falcioni, "Malatesta, Pandolfo," in *Dizionario Biografico degli Italiani*, vol. 68, 2007; online reference: https://www.treccani.it/enciclopedia/pandolfo-malatesta_res-6bc9123b-394c-11dd-904a-0016357eee51_(Dizionario-Biografico)/. Pandolfo's sporadic returns in 1503, 1522, and 1528 make it unlikely that he was committed to fulfilling Rainiero's wishes, especially since Violante seems to have died not long after leaving Rimini.

32 Campana, 1862, p. 423 note 45.

33 The restorers' reports can be found in the present volume. Before these, see G. C. F. Villa, in *Giovanni Bellini,* exhibition catalog (Scuderie del Quirinale, Rome, 30 September, 2008– 11 January, 2009), ed. by M. Lucco and G. C. F. Villa, Cinisello Balsamo, 2008, pp. 178–80 cat. 14, containing a stimulating discussion on the underdrawing in relation to other works by Bellini.

34 See on this the postponing of the dating to 1470 supported by Humfrey and proposed, separately, also by Calogero, 2025, p. 126, both with previous bibliography.

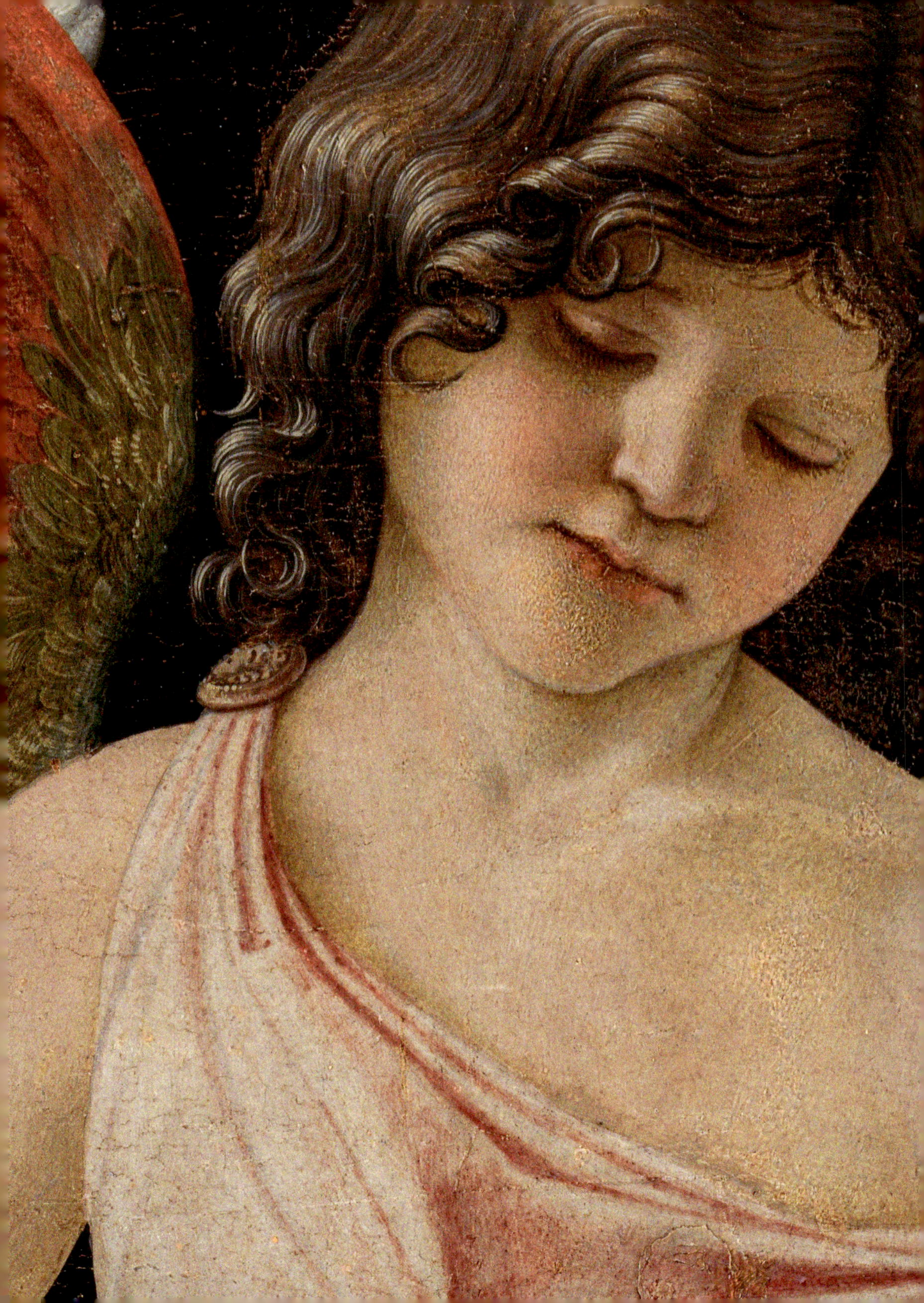

Giovanni Bellini's *Pietà* in Rimini from the Nineteenth Century to the Present Day: From "Precious Gem" to Icon "with Promotional Value"

Giulio Zavatta

For many centuries, Giovanni Bellini's *Pietà* (*Dead Christ supported by Four Angels*) was considered the greatest masterpiece among the paintings in Rimini (fig. 1). However, notwithstanding its importance, the earliest references we have, from Rainerio Migliorati's will of 1499[1] to Vasari's mentions in the two editions of his *Vite*,[2] have been unable to provide conclusive evidence on the commissioning and history of the painting. In some cases, they also have seemed imprecise or even contradictory, leading some experts to speculate that they might have been referring to other works altogether. What remains certain is that the Rimini panel is a masterpiece, a great work that has been almost unanimously praised throughout the centuries.

In 1616, Raffaele Adimari described it as "a beautiful painting of a *Pietà* by Giovanni Bellino, a very famous painter of his time, and esteemed as something excellent and of great value."[3] His praise is echoed in all extant sources, from Rimini and elsewhere. In the eighteenth century, Giovanni Francesco Marcheselli, in *Pitture di Rimini*, praised the author as the "famous Giovan Bellino, master of the great Titian," adding that the painting was "well-preserved."[4] Other eighteenth-century authors, such as Costa,[5] Battaglini,[6] and Algarotti,[7] with alternating opinions, bear witness to the presence of the painting where it had already been seen by Vasari and Adimari, namely in the sacristy of the Church of San Francesco

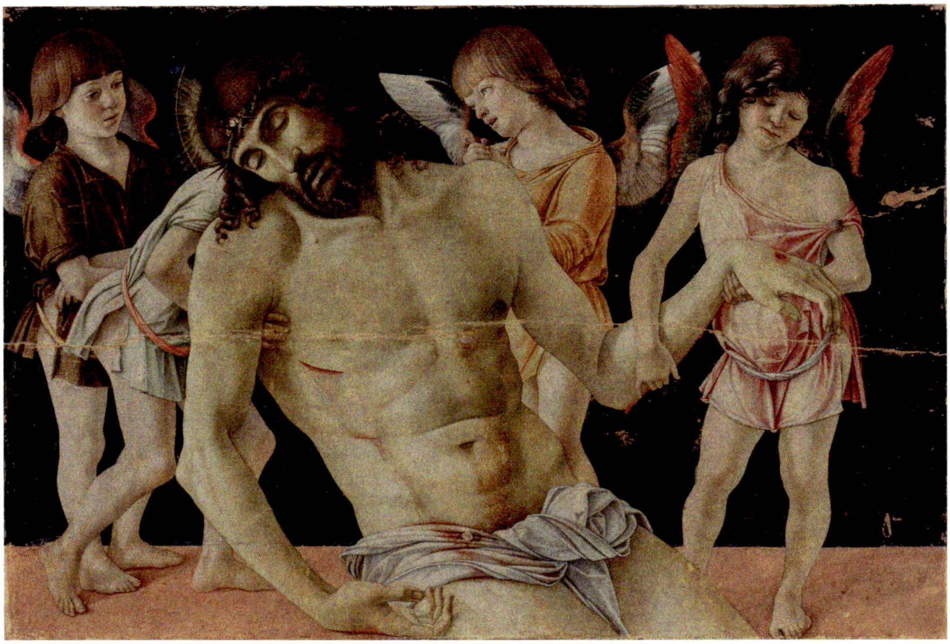

1
Giovanni Bellini, *Pietà*, before restoration, Rimini, Museo della Città "Luigi Tonini"

in Rimini (or Tempio Malatestiano). It has been hypothesized that the work remained in this location also during the Napoleonic requisitions, as it does not appear in the confiscation records.

The presence of the panel in the sacristy of the cathedral is mentioned also in a list of paintings found in the churches of Rimini compiled by the painter Marco Capizucchi in 1805.[8] In the two *Almanacs of the Rubicone Department* published in 1811 and 1812, under the heading "public museums," the Pinacoteca of Rimini is not yet listed.[9] In the survey made for the second volume, nine "paintings to be assigned to the Town" are mentioned, with a Tintoretto as the main work,[10] but without any explicit mention of Bellini's *Pietà*.[11] Unfortunately, the documentation on the library and museum for the following years is incomplete, and the documents preserved in the Gambalunga Library in Rimini make no mention of the painting in the years following the Napoleonic period.[12]

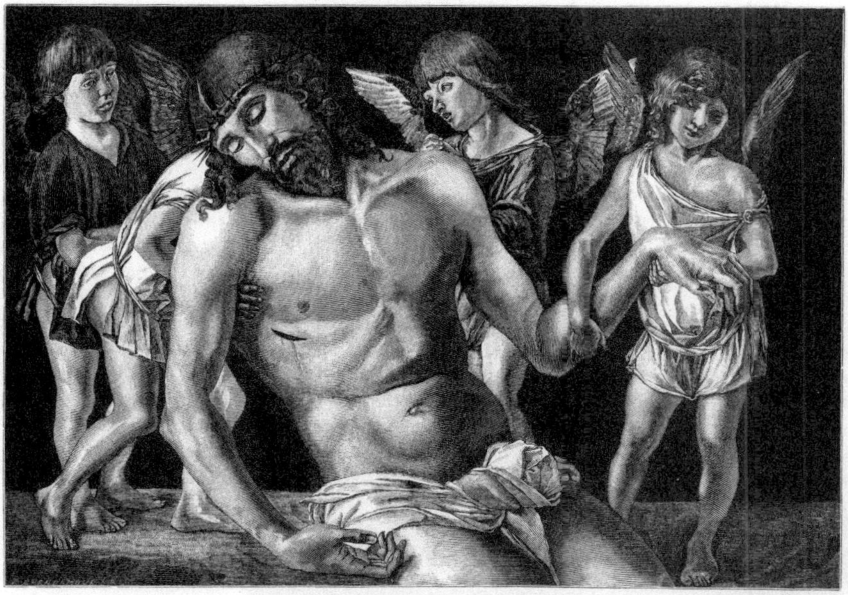

2
Giovanni Bellini, *Pietà – Palazzo Comunale di Rimini*, engraving (from C.F.A. von Lützow, *Die Kunstschätze Italiens*, 1884)

In a *List of noteworthy paintings contained in the churches of the Municipality of Rimini*[13] compiled in 1851, the presence of the painting in the sacristy of the cathedral is no longer mentioned. In Otto Mündler's travel diaries,[14] in 1857 the work is attested for the first time in the town hall (fig. 2), and the location is confirmed in Michelangelo Gualandi's 1861 surveys[15] (who thought it could be easily purchased, valuing it at 900 scudi: "given the lack of interest that the Town of Rimini has in these and other minor paintings of which a room is full, it seems to me that it would not be difficult to enter into negotiations") and in 1864 in Luigi Tonini's *Guide*[16]. In an undated manuscript, probably from the mid-nineteenth century, the same Tonini lists the painting as no. 12, among the twenty paintings preserved in the town hall with the following notation: "Giambellino. Panel depicting Christ taken down from the cross, with angels supporting him: a highly praised work, mentioned by Vasari, p. 468. It deserves to be cleaned and varnished."[17]

Tonini's note is the first mention of any problems with the painting, but the reference is solely to the deterioration of the varnish and no mention is made of the horizontal crack that was to become the focus of subsequent restorations. On the other hand, Luigi Tonini, as is well known, had little sympathy for restoration work, as stated in a letter to Bartolomeo Podestà: "I have always been more afraid of the bad restorations carried out in the present times than of the damage caused by the ravages of time."[18] In 1877, Carlo Tonini—Luigi's son and his successor as director of the library—drew up a list of the paintings in the Rimini Town Hall, which included a "No. 5 Dead Christ with several little angels supporting him / Giovan Bellino, a notable work in his early style / condition: good."[19]

Given this contradictory information, we cannot be sure of the condition of the painting at the time it was examined by restorer Filippo Fiscali, who was in contact with Cavalcaselle,[20] the only expert who questioned Bellini's authorship of the *Pietà*, suggesting Francesco Zaganelli as an alternative.[21] Between 1885 and 1886, Fiscali was commissioned by the Ministry to restore several works in Rimini, including those by Veronese and Bitino da Faenza in San Giuliano and one by Vasari in Scolca. In addition, he also entrusted with the maintenance of the paintings in the Municipal Gallery.[22] We know for certain that he worked on Bellini's panel because on June 28, 1883, the sub-prefect of Rimini wrote a dispatch on the "repairs to the paintings existing in the Town Hall of Rimini," also mentioning the "panel by Giambellino [Giovanni Bellini] depicting a passion."[23] At this stage, Carlo Tonini probably decided to consult an "art expert," the Rimini painter Guglielmo Bilancioni, from whom he expected to receive a "detailed note of the repairs he considered necessary."[24] Bilancioni, however, did not visit Rimini for a long time, the report was consequently delayed and is unfortunately not extant. The information is interesting, however, in that it shows how, at a local level, painters were still considered the best experts, while at the ministerial level, preference was given to people with more specific professional skills in restoration.

The Bellini painting remained in the town hall until 1924, when it was moved to the new pinacoteca (the municipal art gallery) that had been opened in the former convent of San Francesco. On this occasion, as

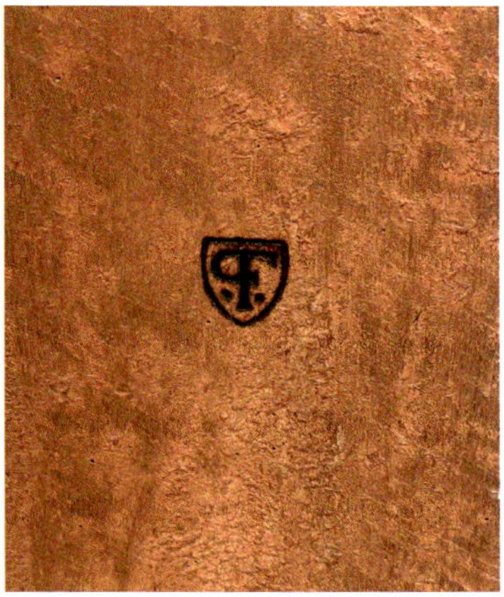

3
Restorer Pompeo Felisati's stamp mark, applied in 1924 on the back of Domenico Ghirlandaio's altarpiece at the Museo della Città di Rimini 'Luigi Tonini"

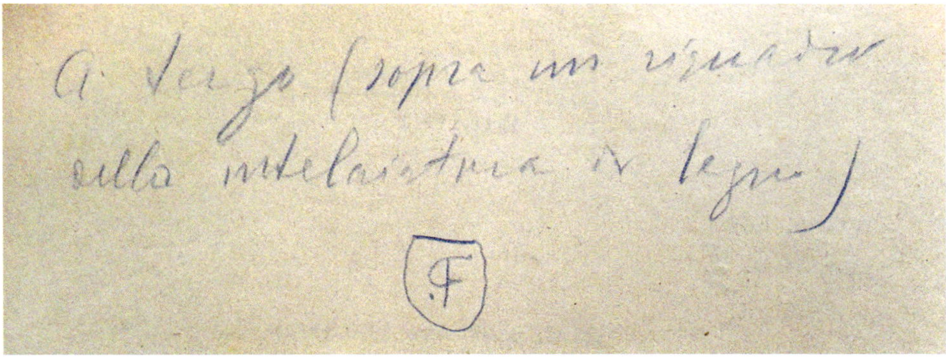

4
Rubbing by Carlo Lucchesi of a stamp on Bellini's *Pietà* panel, Rimini, Biblioteca Gambalunga, Archivio Biblioteca, 1929

recalled by the director of pinacoteca and library Aldo Francesco Massera, Pompeo Felisati carried out a successful and much-appreciated restoration of Ghirlandaio's altarpiece, generally viewed as a twin of Bellini's *Pietà*, discovering four Malatesta figures beneath the repainting.[25] On this occasion, Felisati affixed his stamp (the crossed initials "PF") on the back of the panel (fig. 3). The same symbol was noted by Carlo Lucchesi, Massera's successor as director, "on the wooden frame" of Bellini's *Pietà* at the time of its first shipment to London (fig. 4), discussed below.[26] It is therefore likely that before the opening of the pinacoteca, Felisati worked also on the Bellini panel, as suggested by a 1924 report, in which the condition of the panel is described as "good" as a result of "some minor restoration."[27] Be as it may, as Massera himself recalls, in 1924, the *Pietà* was moved to the pinacoteca, in a small room at the end of the exhibition, together with some "primitives":

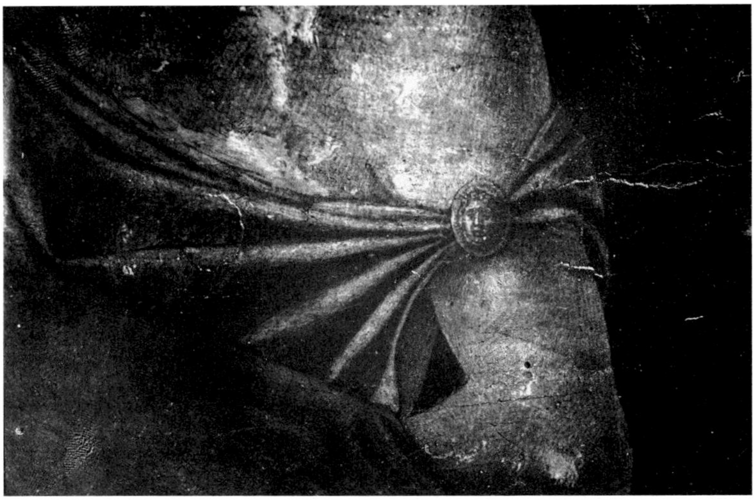

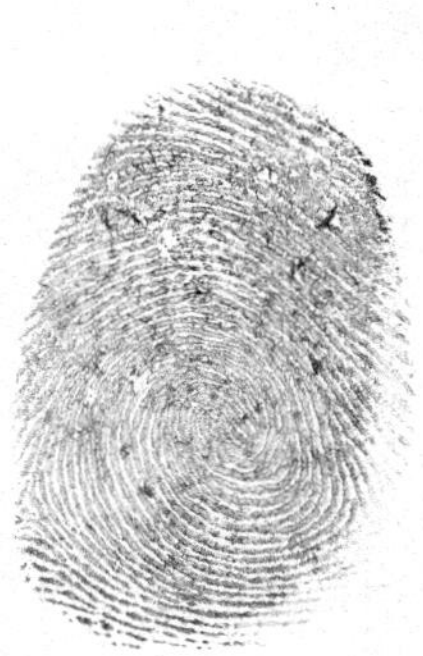

5
Giovanni Bellini, *Pietà*, detail, attached to Carlo Lucchesi's letter to Mayor Pietro Palloni, Rimini, Biblioteca Gambalunga, Archivio Biblioteca, October 1, 1929 (prot. no. 457)

6
Giovanni Bellini, *Pietà*, detail with Carlo Lucchesi's fingerprint, attached to Carlo Lucchesi's letter to Mayor Pietro Palloni, Rimini, Biblioteca Gambalunga, Archivio Biblioteca, October 1, 1929 (prot. no. 457)

7
Sheet with comparative imprint affixed by Carlo Lucchesi, attached to Carlo Lucchesi's letter to Mayor Pietro Palloni, Rimini, Biblioteca Gambalunga, Archivio Biblioteca, October 1, 1929 (prot. no. 457)

> Finally, the two smaller rooms at the end of the long corridor contain the gems of the Pinacoteca: one, Giovanni Bellini's *Pietà* with some primitives . . .; the other, the superb composition commissioned as an *ex voto* by Pandolfo IV Malatesta to Domenico Ghirlandaio. Both masterpieces have been lovingly taken care of.[28]

The painting's move to the new museum coincided with the beginning of a much more eventful life: after centuries in which it had traveled only the short distance between the Tempio Malatestiano and the town hall, the last hundred years have been characterized by a series of appearances in exhibitions in Italy and abroad, which have unfortunately resulted also in a radical and possibly irreversible change in appearance. This new life began in 1929, when the painting was shipped outside Rimini for the first time on loan to the *Italian Exhibition* in London. For the recently opened museum in Rimini, the request made by the Prefect of Forlì and directly supported by Mussolini, came as a surprise and caused no little apprehension. On September 16, 1929, the then director Carlo Lucchesi communicated his "great anxiety" to the *podestà* Pietro Palloni, due to his having "had to remove this priceless art treasure from its secure home and, to some extent, entrust it to the whims of fate."[29] Lucchesi went on to express his hope that "the most effective measures would be taken to safeguard and protect the painting." The news spread quickly throughout the city, so much so that a week later Lucchesi himself reported to the *podestà*: "I will not conceal from you, as is my duty, that the news (which spread, I do not know how) has caused great concern among the city's art lovers, who adore this gem (unique and true) of the Pinacoteca with boundless love."[30] Lucchesi then asked for permission to take himself some precautions, fearing that during its long absence from Rimini, a copy of the painting might be made and returned to the city in place of the original. He had some details photographed, evidencing signs of wear and tear that were not easily replicable, and decided to "place a small, almost imperceptible mark of recognition, known only to us," namely the fingerprint of his thumb, in some specific points on the edges of the panel, which were also photographed. The director then copied his fingerprint also on a small sheet of paper, for future comparison (figs. 5–7).[31]

All the secret precautions taken by the suspicious Lucchesi risked being vanified when the curator of the London exhibition, Ettore Modigliani, announced that he had obtained some funds for the restoration of the panel, to be carried out at the Pinacoteca of Brera in Milan, where the masterpieces destined for Burlington House were being assembled before being shipped. The restoration was necessary because the colors were altered in the center of the panel, where Felisati had previously carried out the retouching. In addition, the panel appeared to be unstable. Overcoming Lucchesi's resistance, who was concerned that his "signs of recognition" would be erased,[32] a major restoration was carried out by Mauro Pellicioli.[33] From a letter by Modigliani, we learn that the system of stabilizing panels with "cumbersome and extremely dangerous fixed bars" was now considered obsolete. Instead, a plan was made to replace it with a more elastic cradling: a "sliding grid."[34] In addition, the previous restoration, made with pigments that had quickly altered, was to be corrected, retouching the central area again to hide the large crack in the panel. On this issue, Antonio Morassi's testimony[35] in the context of the London exhibition is the first explicit information we have: "the panel was split in half horizontally and badly retouched."[36] An exceptional photograph published in the magazine *The Sphere*[37] (fig. 8) documents the restoration work carried out in Milan.

The loan for the *Italian Exhibition* was a success for the Rimini painting, the more so after Charles Holmes declared the panel, now brought to the world's attention alongside Botticelli's works from the Uffizi, to be the most beautiful of Bellini's various *Pietàs*: "the *Pietà* of Rimini is the finest of its kind."[38] When the painting returned to Rimini, Lucchesi—after finding the fingerprints and checking whether they matched—reported to the *podestà* that the work had returned "more resplendent thanks to the cleaning" and with a "modern and rational frame with which it has been secured" (fig. 9).[39]

After being seen by more than half a million visitors in London, the *Pietà* of Rimini, returned thus to the humdrum of a provincial town, where museum visitors barely amounted to a thousand per year, albeit displayed in a prominent position in the pinacoteca alongside Ghirlandaio's altarpiece.[40] However, the international success did bring about a surge of interest even in Rimini, which led Carlo Lucchesi, a few days after the return, to ask the

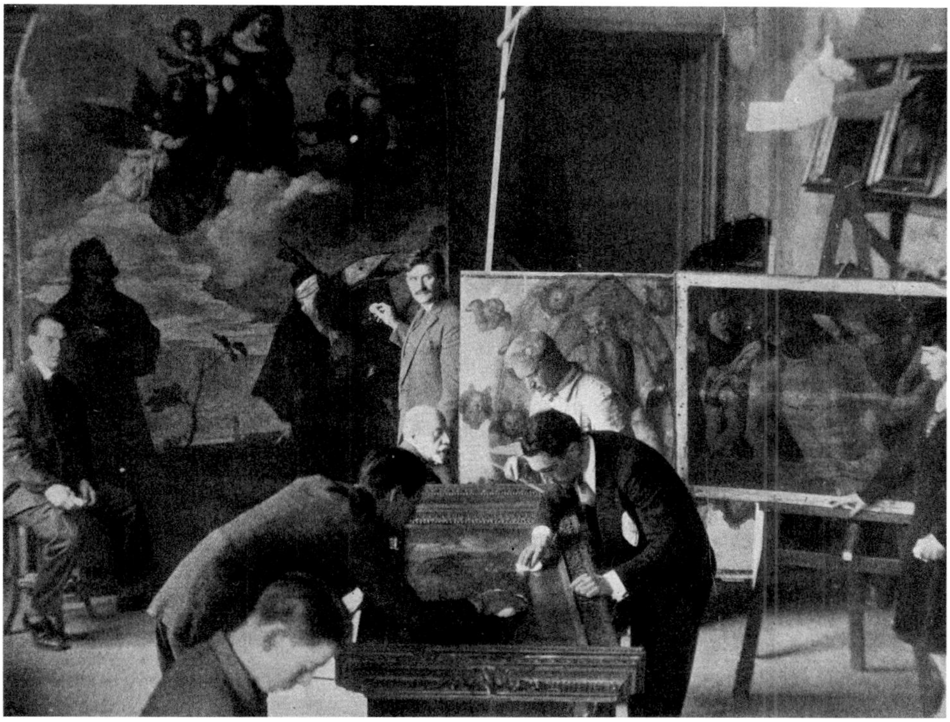

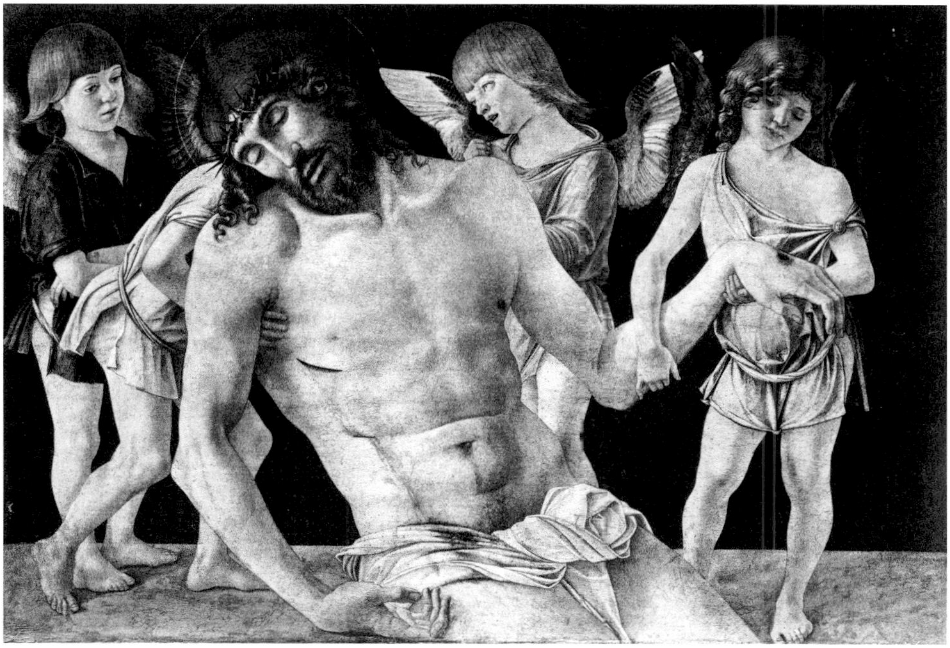

8
Paintings awaiting shipment to London in the restoration workshop of the Pinacoteca di Brera, Milan, in *The Sphere*, November 30, 1929

9
Giovanni Bellini, *Pietà*, after Pellicioli's restoration, 1930

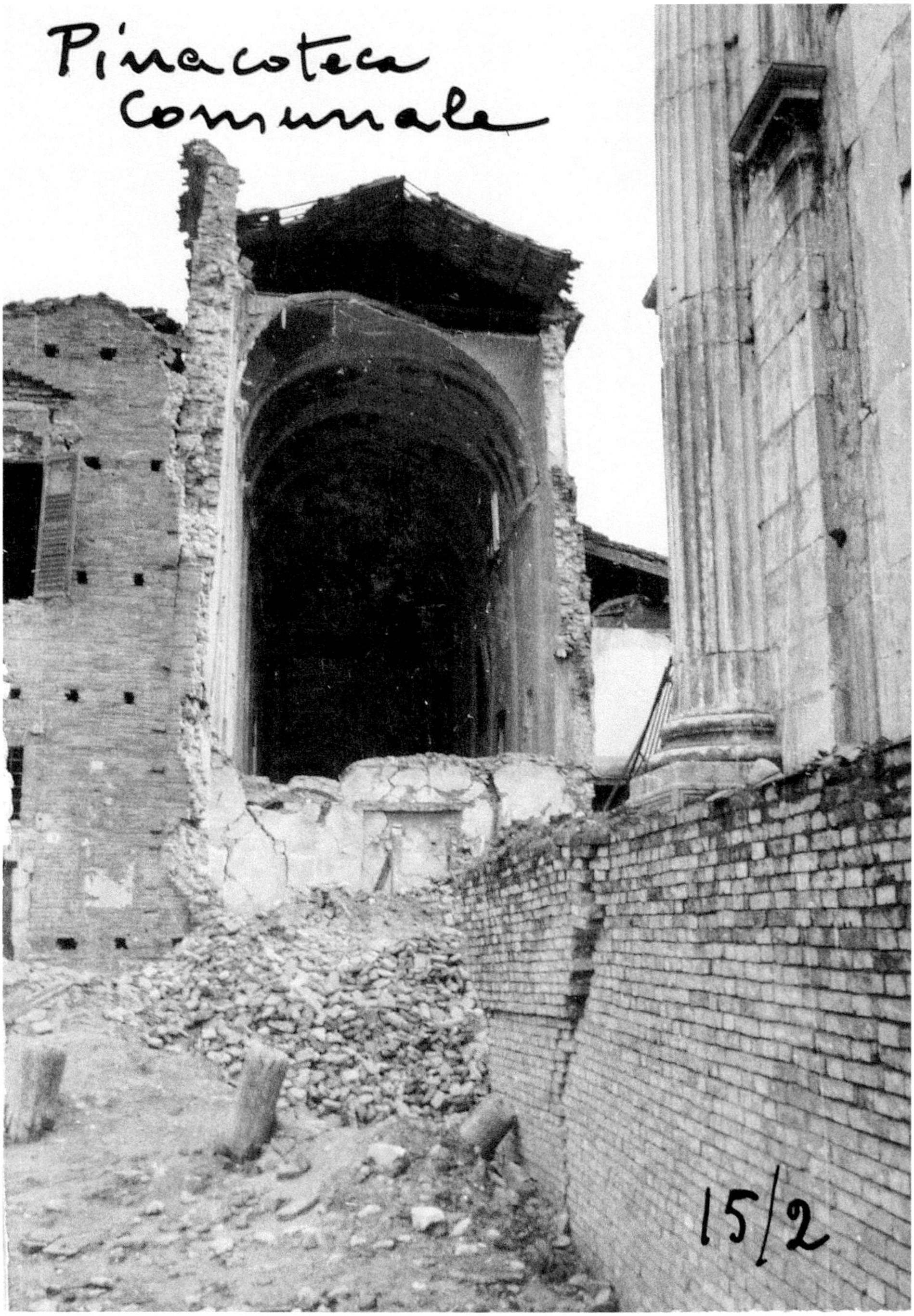

10
The Pinacoteca di Rimini after the bombings of World War II, Rimini, Biblioteca Gambalunga, Photographic Archive (inv. no. Afp004535.02.15)

municipal administration for funds to build barriers to protect Bellini and Ghirlandaio, since:

> Unfortunately, due to lack of space, the two precious paintings by Giambellino and Ghirlandaio are located within easy reach, and visitors often get too close to them in order to better observe and admire them, touching them with their faces or, worse, with their hands, despite the warnings from the custodian.[41]

For this reason, permission was granted to:

> Have a small, simple, and inexpensive iron gate built around each of the two precious paintings by Giambellino and Ghirlandaio, which, while keeping visitors at a safe distance from the paintings so as not to damage or spoil them, would not at the same time hinder their observation.[42]

This precaution was not altogether effective, as noted by the Bolognese superintendent Luigi Corsini who, when visiting Rimini on July 1, 1930, observed that the small gate was unable to entirely restrain the public, and in particular the painter Aldo Roncaglia, who, in making a copy of the *Pietà*, had been "getting too close to the original," risking "an unpredictable accident [that] could cause damage to the precious work."[43]

Another problem was that the museum did not have any means to regulate the temperature of the building. In July 1931, a heat wave caused some damage to Giuliano da Rimini's polyptych, located in the same room as Bellini's *Pietà*. However, Lucchesi was able to reassure the *podestà* that the precious Renaissance panel had not suffered, thanks to the restoration performed by Pellicioli (which Lucchesi had tried in every way to prevent):

> [in the case of] 'Giambellino', I think the new adjustments made in Milan before it was sent to the London Exhibition proved truly providential, because, thanks to the balancing and compensating between the various parts of the frame, despite the occasional slight knock or creak, the precious panel shows no sign of damage.[44]

The painting remained in the new Pinacoteca of Rimini only for another ten years, until the outbreak of World War II. On June 10, 1940, the *commissario prefettizio*, temporarily in charge of the town, informed Carlo Lucchesi that the superintendent of Bologna had requested that Rimini's main works of art be urgently transferred to a safer location, which in the case of the museum, meant immediately moving Bellini's *Pietà*, along with Ghirlandaio's altarpiece, Giuliano da Rimini's polyptych, *Diotallevi Crucifix*, and the tapestries.[45] At first, the precious panel was moved to the Convento delle Grazie, in the hills of Rimini, and then again in 1944 to Torricella di Novafeltria, where Guido Mattei Gentili had made his home available as a safehouse. Rimini's precious artistic treasures made it through the World War II unscathed, and on September 28, 1944, Carlo Lucchesi was able to communicate the following to the secretary general of the town of Rimini:

> I am pleased to assure you that the precious deposit entrusted to me is entirely safe, and I am also safe, as this area of the Marecchia Valley has been spared the horrors of war. We thank God for inspiring us to bring so many treasures up here. If only we had brought the rest too![46]

Bellini's *Pietà* was safe, but the pinacoteca established in the former convent of San Francesco only twenty years earlier had been destroyed (fig. 10). As early as 1946, it was therefore decided to use some rooms on the first floor of the Gambalunga Library as a temporary gallery. The inauguration, however, took place only on September 5, 1948, with the exhibition of a "forest of paintings, which to some may appear confusing," as Carlo Lucchesi forewarned in his speech.[47] The works from the museum of Rimini, including Bellini's painting, found a suitable museum location only in the 1990s, almost fifty years after the war, when they were placed in a former Jesuit convent. From the immediate post-war period and the long "temporary" stay in the library, there remain some photographs from the Minghini collection which also show a later location within the library that was perhaps no longer "confusing" but still appears quite cramped (fig. 11). The *Pietà* appears placed near Ghirlandaio's altarpiece, as witnessed also by a list compiled in 1960 by director Mario Zuffa, describing a great number of works concentrated in just four rooms and two corridors of the library.[48]

Returning to the years following the end of World War II, Bellini's painting was sent to Bologna for a "correction of the chromatic altera-

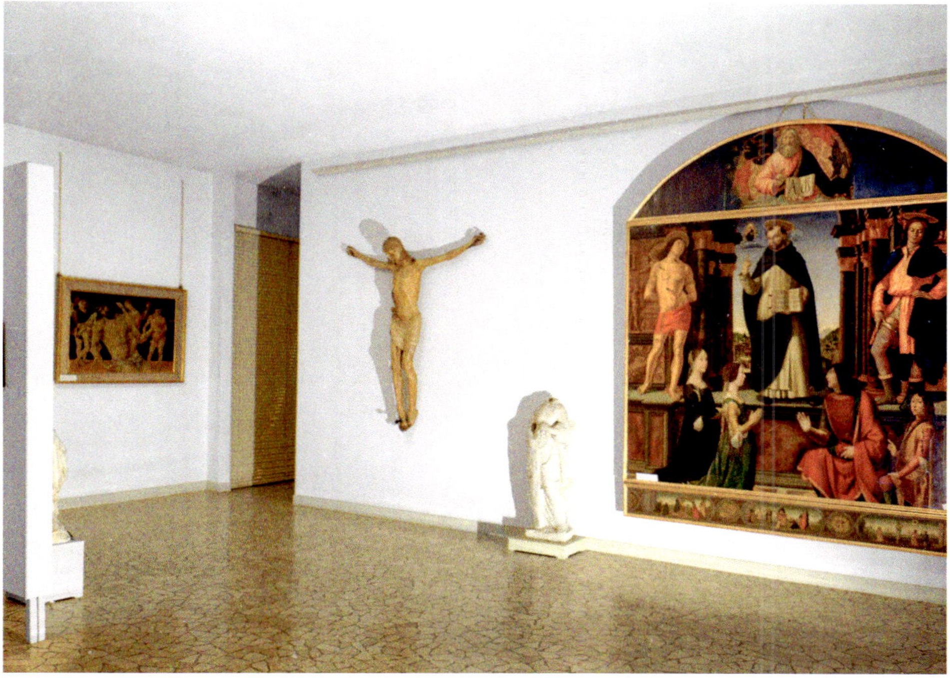

11
Bellini's Pietà and Ghirlandaio's Pala Malatestiana in the halls of the Biblioteca Gambalunga, in Rimini, Photographic Archive, 1972 (inv. no. MIN 06413.001)

tion that had gradually occurred following the restoration it underwent when it was sent to the exhibition of Italian masterpieces in London,"[49] as attested by documents dating back to 1949, when a new request to borrow the painting for the Giovanni Bellini exhibition held at the Doge's Palace in Venice was forwarded to the Superintendency in Bologna.[50] This time, the request was backed by a polite letter from the mayor of Venice, Giaquinto, who emphasized the "critical and public success" of previous exhibitions in Venice, as well as all the "guarantees of custody and perfect organization" demonstrated on such occasions.[51] Superintendent Sorrentino approved the loan, but made it conditional on the "necessary restoration of the panel itself,"[52] which had not yet been carried out in Bologna. From Rimini, Lucchesi, mindful of the events in London (where, as is well known, the ship carrying the works of art encountered a storm while crossing the English Channel), requested a substantial increase in the value insured and coverage for transport, even though the danger to the painting could seem "unlikely and remote."[53] According to Lucchesi, in Venice too, as before the exhibition in London, the painting was "masterfully retouched and cleaned by Prof. Pelliccioli [*sic*]."[54] Mention of the intervention is found in the documentation of the exhibition, in Pelliccioli's accounts: "3° Rimini. 'La Pietà,' old registers, altered restorations, color balancing. 12,000 lire."[55]

After its successful foray in Venice, the painting was thus now back in Rimini on October 18, 1949, "admirably rejuvenated."[56] But this was not the only legacy of the Venetian expedition. From the correspondence between Lucchesi and the Venetian organization we know that the director of the Pinacoteca of Rimini must have been concerned that the painting's frame might be removed. As is well known, at the exhibition curated by Scarpa and Pallucchini all the frames that were not contemporary with the paintings were removed, with the sole exception of Bellini's *Pietà*.[57] A document from the Superintendency of the Galleries of Bologna confirms this:

> As for the painting, it was framed with a small light wood frame surrounded by a strip of light-colored canvas. This is how the entire exhibition was set up, in a modern style, according to the wishes of the entire Advisory Committee. However, the Rimini painting is the only one that has its own wooden strip.[58]

Lucchesi too, after visiting the exhibition, confirmed that "the painting was displayed without a frame, enclosed only by a small strip of light wood, with a wide band of ivory-white canvas around it."[59] All in all, Lucchesi appreciated this solution, as suggested also by the fact that he asked and obtained that the panel be returned with the above frame,[60] which is probably the one visible in Minghini's photograph. Lucchesi makes no mention whatsoever of the famous architect's ideas for the exhibition, despite Pallucchini's suggestion that "exhibition experiences are very useful and can benefit museums themselves,"[61] nor did he seem troubled by the controversy raging among Pallucchini, Brandi, and Longhi regarding the quality of Pellicioli's restorations.[62]

In the summer of 1950, the panel was again exhibited for the *Mostra malatestiana*, which was held in the Gambalunga Library where the painting was kept. After this there twenty years went by, during which the panel remained peacefully in the limbo of the little-visited rooms of the library. The only novelty during this period came in 1962, when Augusto Campana finally published Migliorati's will, mentioned at beginning, which he had discovered fifteen years earlier.[63] In both the publication and in his notes, Campana discussed also the apocryphal signature scratched in the lower right-hand corner, stating that it had never been mentioned in previous studies. In truth, as Campana later discovered in correspondence with the Rimini painter Gino Ravaioli, the latter had already cited its presence in a 1949 publication,[64] and had also provided a transcription—albeit incorrect— an error that, as Ravaioli himself explained, was due to the "fact that before the painting was cleaned" by Pellicioli in Venice "the signature was unclear and difficult to read."[65]

The last documented extensive restoration was carried out in 1969 by Otello Caprara and Ottorino Nonfarmale, exactly twenty years after the last maintenance session, and entailed the rather extreme decision of transferring the painting from the old wooden panel to canvas. As early as 1964, the superintendent of Bologna, Cesare Gnudi, had already informed the mayor of Rimini, Giulio Cesare Santini, that he had obtained co-financing from the ministry, with an equal sum to be contributed by the town, due to the "urgent need" to intervene on "the most precious paintings in the Pinacoteca."[66] The restoration project called for following: "Restoration of the wooden support, reduction of convexity, cradling. Cleaning, general consolidation, pictorial retouching and reintegration."[67]

The work, however, was evidently not carried out at the time, and so five years later a new project arrived from Gnudi entitled "Wood restoration and removal of wood material from a painting on wood depicting 'Pietà' by Giovanni Bellini located in the Pinacoteca of Rimini," to which a dramatic technical report was attached. As part of an effort to "verify the intrinsic capacity of the wooden support to withstand the passage of time and still provide adequate protection to the painted surface," it was noted that:

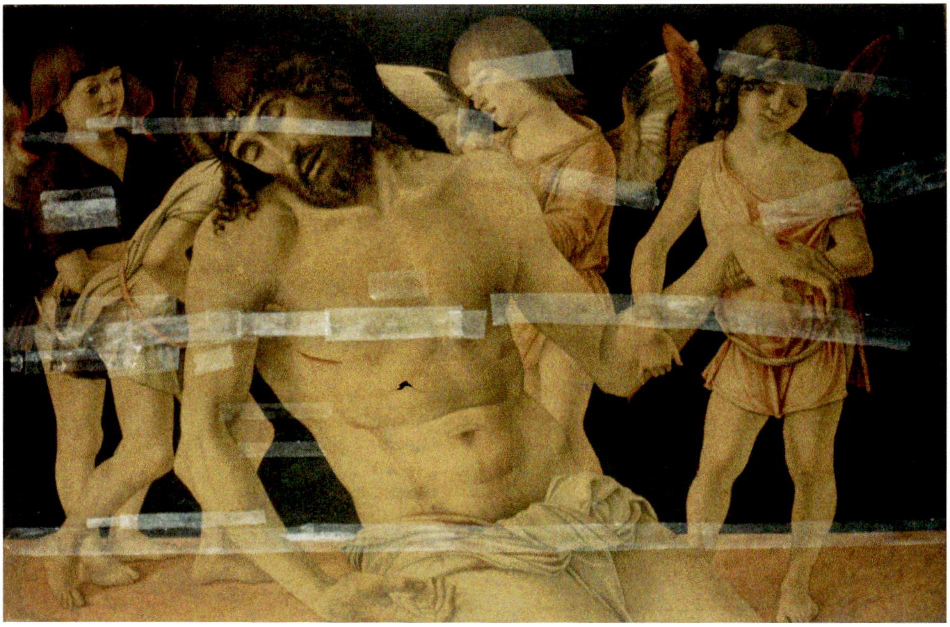

12
Giovanni Bellini, *Pietà*, condition of the painting during Nonfarmale's restoration

> the sapwood is threatened by parasites, which have worked undisturbed, mainly because they are protected by a "Florentine" cradling that has served no other purpose than to conceal the degradation of the material that was taking place beneath the latticework.

The passage tells us that the "modern" system used by Pellicioli in 1929 was a "Florentine-style" cradling, that is a very tight sliding grid (as documented by Sara Masinelli in the present volume) and that this was considered the reason behind the irreparable deterioration of the original panel (fig. 12). A later message dated July 10, 1969,[68] certified the tragic results of the ancient painting's twentieth-century restoration history:

> Every effort has been made to consolidate the wooden support of this painting, which is the sole but unfortunately very serious cause of the deterioration of the painted surface itself. [...]

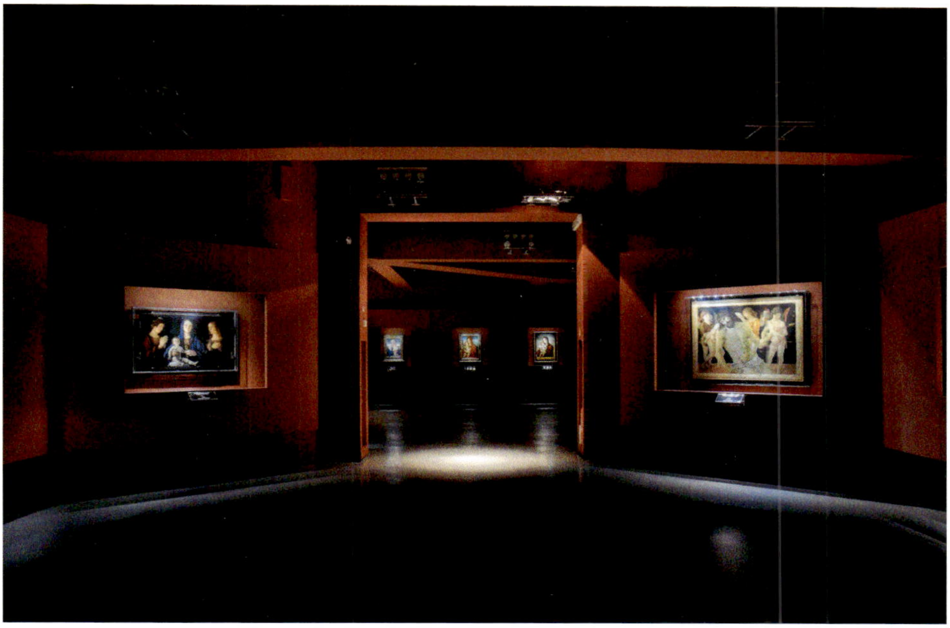

13
Installation view of the Bellini exhibition at the Scuderie del Quirinale in Rome (2008), with the *Pietà* from the Museo della Città "Luigi Tonini", Rimini

> Unfortunately, this work—although carried out with the utmost skill and expertise—has not been sufficient to halt the negative process underway.

This led to the final decision of transferring "the painting from the old dilapidated panel to canvas."[69] This material change led also to a change in the attitude of the authorities, who deemed that now that the painting was on canvas instead of a fragile panel, it could be safely transported.

The twentieth-century history of the *Pietà* of Rimini continued to be rather eventful in the following years. In 1990, a new home was found for it in the present pinacoteca, inaugurated on July 12 in an ex-Jesuit convent. Previously, the *Pietà* had been selected for two exhibitions in Rimini. The first one, *Sigismondo Pandolfo Malatesta and his Time*, was held in 1970 (though the painting, while listed in the catalog, was not ultimately exhibited, probably because it was still undergoing restoration).[70] The second exhibition, *Painting in Rimini between the Gothic and Renaissance periods*, was held in

1979.[71] After remaining undisturbed for another twenty years, the delicate painting was then loaned for no less than thirteen exhibitions, between 2000 and 2019 (fig. 13).[72] To this we can add a loan that was granted and subsequently denied for the 2012 exhibition in Rimini, *From Vermeer to Kandinsky. Masterpieces from the world's museums in Rimini,* and another that was also revoked for the exhibition *Treasures of Italy*, as part of the Expo 2015 in Milan. In the case of the Expo 2015, the official reason for the loan was the same of all the more recent ones: "the promotional value that could accrue to the Museums of Rimini."[73] The news of the loan sparked a controversy in the press,[74] in which doubts were cast on whether the work could be safely moved. The response was that the canvas had been reinforced during the 1969 Nonfarmale restoration with the addition of a fiberglass support, which would keep it stable and safe during any transfer, also "given the optimal conditions of conservation"[75] [*sic*] of the work. It was added that "the level of transportation safety and the parameters and conditions of the exhibition are such that the preservation of the work is absolutely guaranteed."[76] One must note that, despite the confidence of the authorities in charge, in 2019, only four years later, while being shipped from London to Berlin, the *Pietà* suffered "alterations" and small tears to the painted surface due to "the adhesion of the packaging material."[77]

Summarizing, Bellini's precious work, after being peacefully housed in the Tempio Malatestiano for centuries, began a new and much more eventful life, starting with its transfer in the nineteenth century to the first Pinacoteca of Rimini. Between the end of the nineteenth century and 1969, it underwent at least five documented restorations, some of them very invasive, after which it was subject to practically no maintenance for more than fifty years, making it probably Bellini's work most in need of intervention. Its "exhibition life," in particular, began in London in 1930 and was initially always accompanied by restoration work, only to intensify precisely in the period when the painting was no longer being maintained, with a frenetic series of exhibitions that was halted only by the arrival of the 2019 pandemic. Today, thanks to the generous intervention of Venetian Heritage, the "gem" of the Pinacoteca of Rimini is finally being restored, in the knowledge, I hope, that every restoration in its past has been a crucial material as well as historical and critical moment in its history. The importance of the *Pietà* of Rimini requires that special care be taken, carefully weighing the pros and cons of any intervention, as well as the possible consequences over time. A time that in the last decades has become far too fast-paced and must now be slowed down to a rhythm that will ensure the future safety of this precious and troubled masterpiece of the Renaissance.

1 A. Campana, *Notizie sulla 'Pietà' riminese di Giovanni Bellini*, in *Scritti di Storia dell'arte in onore di Mario Salmi*, ed. by V. Martinelli and F.M. Aliberti, Rome, 1962, vol. II, p. 419.

2 G. Vasari, *Le vite de' più eccellenti architetti, pittori et scultori italiani, da Cimabue insino a' tempi nostri. Nell'edizione per i tipi di Lorenzo Torrentino*, Florence 1550, Turin, 1886, p. 437; G. Vasari, *Le vite de' più eccellenti architetti, pittori et scultori italiani, da Cimabue insino a' tempi nostri*, Florence 1568, ed. by G. Milanesi, Florence 1878–1885, vol. III, p. 170.

3 R. Adimari, *Sito riminese di Raffaele Adimari da Rimino dove si tratta della città, & sue parti, & come si potesse ampliare, & fin' dove arrivano li suoi confini da tutte le parti di terra, et in particolare, di tutte le chiese, & cose ecclesiastiche, che sono nella città, e fuori di essa*, Brescia, 1616, p. 68.

4 C. F. Marcheselli, *Pitture di Rimini*, ed. by P. G. Pasini, Bologna, 1972, pp. 61–62.

5 G. B. Costa, "Il Tempio di San Francesco in Rimino," in *Miscellanea di varia letteratura*, Lucca, 1765, vol. V, p. 50.

6 A. Battaglini, "Della corte letteraria di Sigismondo Malatesta," in *Basinii Parmensis opera praestantiora*, Rimini, 1794, vol. II, t. 1, p. 68.

7 G. G. Bottari, S. Ticozzi, *Raccolta di lettere sulla pittura, scultura ed architettura scritte da' più celebri personaggi dei secoli XV, XVI, e XVII*, Milan 1822, vol. VII, p. 489.

8 G. Zavatta, "1805: l'anno fortunato di Marco Capizucchi e l'elenco dei migliori quadri nelle chiese di Rimini," *Romagna arte e storia*, no. 115, 2020, pp. 37–54, in particular pp. 45, 50.

9 *Almanacco del Dipartimento del Rubicone per l'anno 1811*, Rimini, 1811, p. 162; *Almanacco del Dipartimento del Rubicone per l'anno bisestile 1812*, Forlì, 1812, p. 362.

10 The painting is *San Domenico presenta la regola al Papa*, see P. G. Pasini, *La Pinacoteca di Rimini*, Cinisello Balsamo, 1983, p. 29.

11 Archivio di Stato di Rimini, Archivio Storico del Comune, busta 248 (1812) titolo X (Pubblica Istruzione), no. 256 (list of paintings and possessions belonging to the Town of Rimini, August 20, 1812).

12 Rimini, Biblioteca Gambalunga, Archivio Biblioteca, envelope I (1822–1879).

13 *Elenco delle pitture di merito contenute nelle Chiese del Comune di Rimini*, Archivio di Stato di Rimini, Archivio Storico del Comune, envelope 759 (1851).

14 J. Anderson, "Otto Mündler and his Travel Diary," in *The travel diaries of Otto Mundler 1855–1858*, edited by C. Togneri Dowd and by J. Anderson (*The fifty-first volume of the Walpole Society*), London, 1985, p. 9.

15 G. Mazzaferro, "Patrimonio indifeso: Opere d'arte e mercato nel viaggio di Michelangelo Gualandi in centro Italia (March 1861)," *Kritiké*, no. 2, 2021, pp. 195–231.

16 L. Tonini, *Guida del forestiere nella città di Rimini*, Rimini, 1864, p. 35; sulla galleria comunale: P. G. Pasini, "La formazione della 'Galleria' comunale e la dispersione delle 'Gallerie' private," in *Storia di Rimini dal 1800 ai giorni nostri. III L'arte e il patrimonio artistico e archeologico*, ed. by P. G. Pasini and M. Zuffa, Rimini, 1978, pp. 148–51; P. G. Pasini, 1983, pp. 12–13, 41–44.

17 Rimini, Biblioteca Gambalunga, Carte Tonini, busta XX.
18 P. G. Pasini, "Restauri ottocenteschi," in *Storia di Rimini*, 1978, p. 151.
19 Rimini, Biblioteca Gambalunga, Carte Tonini, busta XIX, quaderno 1.
20 D. Levi, *Cavalcaselle,* Turin, 1988, pp. 334, 344–53.
21 J. A. Crowe, G. B. Cavalcaselle, *History of Painting in North Italy: Venice, Padua, Vicenza, Verona, Ferrara, Milan, Friuli, Brescia*, London, 1871, vol. I, pp. 190, 194, 601.
22 Pasini, "Restauri ottocenteschi," 1978, p. 152; Pasini, 1983, p. 42; A. Pellicciari, "Conservazione e politica culturale a Rimini e nel suo territorio," in *Il estauro. Intelligenza e progetto*, ed. by A. Stanzani, Bologna 1990, p. 347.
23 Rimini, Biblioteca Gambalunga, Archivio Biblioteca, 1881–1890, fasc. I (1881–1885), letter dated June 28, 1883, from the sub-prefect of Rimini to the director of the library, Carlo Tonini.
24 Rimini, Biblioteca Gambalunga, Archivio Biblioteca, 1881–1890, fasc. I (1881–1885), letter dated October 22, 1883, from Carlo Tonini to the sub-prefect of Rimini.
25 A. F. Massera, "Principi del Rinascimento che rinascono," *Cronache d'arte*, no. I, 1924, pp. 95–101.
26 Rimini, Biblioteca Gambalunga, Archivio Biblioteca, anno 1929, titolo IX (Art Gallery), attached to the packaging documents of October 8, 1929. G. Zavatta, "La Pietà di Rimini di Giovanni Bellini: esposizioni e restauri (1930–2019)," in *"Storia dell'arte" in tempo reale. Previews and ongoing research, insights into current events, discoveries, new readings 2021-22*, ed. by M. Moretti, J. Pezzali, A. Sbrilli, Rome, 2023, p. 214; the same references also in G. Zavatta, "Giovanni Bellini's Pietà di Rimini: exhibitions and restorations (1930–2019)," *Storia dell'arte*, n.s. 2, no. 158, 2022, pp. 26–47.
27 Pasini, 1983, p. 208.
28 A. F. Massera, *Cenni Storici Artistici sul Museo e la Pinacoteca Comunali*, Rimini, 1924, pp. 7–12.
29 Rimini, Biblioteca Gambalunga, Archivio Biblioteca, letter from Carlo Lucchesi to the *podestà* of Rimini Pietro Palloni, September 16, 1929; Zavatta, 2023, p. 206.
30 Rimini, Biblioteca Gambalunga, Archivio Biblioteca, Letter from Carlo Lucchesi to the *podestà* of Rimini Pietro Palloni, September 23, 1929; Zavatta, 2023, p. 206.
31 Ibid. p. 207.
32 Ibid.
33 Ibid., pp. 216–28.
34 Ibid., p. 216.
35 A. Morassi, "La mostra d'arte italiana a Londra," *Emporium*, no. 71, 1930, pp. 131–57.
36 Ibid., p. 142.
37 Zavatta, 2023, p. 214.
38 C. Holmes, "The Italian Exhibition," *The Burlington Magazine*, vol. 56, no. 323, 1930, p. 65.
39 Rimini, Biblioteca Gambalunga, Archivio Biblioteca, letter from Carlo Lucchesi to the *podestà* Pietro Palloni, ref. no. 293, May 22, 1930. Zavatta, 2023, p. 220.
40 C. Valentini, *La nascita della Pinacoteca di Rimini e i suoi primi anni di vita attraverso i documenti della Biblioteca Gambalunga,* PHD thesis, Ca' Foscari University, Venice, supervisor Prof. G. Zavatta, academic year 2024–25, p. 89.
41 Rimini, Biblioteca Gambalunga, Archivio Biblioteca (1930), letter from Carlo Lucchesi to Pietro Palloni, May 22, 1930, Zavatta, 2023, p. 220.
42 Rimini, Biblioteca Gambalunga, Archivio Biblioteca (1930), letter from Pietro Palloni to Carlo Lucchesi, ref. no. 293, May 26, 1930.
43 Valentini, 2024–25, p. 90.
44 Rimini, Biblioteca Gambalunga, Archivio Biblioteca (1931), letter from Carlo Lucchesi to Pietro Palloni, July 25, 1931.
45 Rimini, Biblioteca Gambalunga, Archivio Biblioteca, fasc. "Guerra 1940–1945," letter from the prefectural commissioner (*commissario prefettizio)* to Carlo Lucchesi, June 10, 1940.
46 Rimini, Biblioteca Gambalunga, Archivio Biblioteca, fasc. "Guerra 1940–1945," letter from Carlo Lucchesi to the head secretary of the Town of Rimini, September 28, 1944.
47 C. Lucchesi, "Discorso per la riapertura della Pinacoteca Comunale. Rinascita: risplendono i tesori d'arte," *Il Litorale*, September 20, 1948, p. 2.
48 Pasini, 1983, pp. 225–26.
49 Rimini, Biblioteca Gambalunga, Archivio Biblioteca (1949), Letter from Carlo Lucchesi to G. B. Giaquinto, March 12, 1949, Zavatta, 2023, pp. 224–25.
50 Rimini, Biblioteca Gambalunga, Archivio Biblioteca (1949), letter from G. B. Giaquinto to Antonino Sorrentino, superintendent of the Galleries of Bologna, February 1949; Zavatta, 2023, p. 222.
51 Rimini, Biblioteca Gambalunga, Archivio Biblioteca (1949), letter from G. B. Giaquinto to the mayor and director of the museum of Rimini, February 22, 1949, Zavatta, 2023, p. 222.
52 Rimini, Biblioteca Gambalunga, Archivio Biblioteca (1949), letter from Antonino Sorrentino to G. B. Giaquinto, February 23, 1949.
53 Rimini, Biblioteca Gambalunga, Archivio Biblioteca (1949), letter from Carlo Lucchesi to the mayor of Rimini, March 16, 1949.

54 Rimini, Biblioteca Gambalunga, Archivio Biblioteca (1949), letter from Carlo Lucchesi to the mayor of Rimini, July 11, 1949; Zavatta 2023, p. 226.
55 Archivio Storico del Comune di Venezia, Celestia, *Mostra di Giovanni Bellini,* Miscellaneous 2, letter from Mauro Pellicioli from Milan to the management of the exhibition, August 24, 1949.
56 Rimini, Biblioteca Gambalunga, Archivio Biblioteca (1949), letter from Carlo Lucchesi to the management of the exhibition on Giovanni Bellini in Venice, October 18, 1949; Zavatta 2023, p. 228.
57 *Giovanni Bellini. Catalogo illustrato della mostra*, ed. by R. Pallucchini, Venice, 1949, p. 26; A.C. Cimoli, *Musei effimeri. Allestimenti di mostre in Italia 1949–1963*, Milan, 2007, pp. 37–39.
58 Rimini, Biblioteca Gambalunga, Archivio Biblioteca, Letter from the Superintendency to the Galleries of Bologna, undated and without recipient [but later than June 28, 1949].
59 Rimini, Biblioteca Gambalunga, Archivio Biblioteca (1949), letter from Carlo Lucchesi to the mayor of Rimini, July 11, 1949; Zavatta, 2023, p. 226.
60 Ibid.
61 *Giovanni Bellini. Catalogo illustrato*, 1949, p. 26.
62 C. Brandi, "The Cleaning of Pictures in Relation to Patina, Varnish, and Glazes," *The Burlington Magazine*, vol. 91, no. 556, 1949, pp. 183–88; R. Longhi, "The Giovanni Bellini Exhibition," *The Burlington Magazine*, vol. 91, no. 559, pp. 274–83; S. Rinaldi, "Brandi rimprovera Pallucchini: vernici e velature nei restauri belliniani del 1949," in *Rodolfo Pallucchini: storie, archivi, prospettive critiche,* ed. by C. Lorenzini, Udine, 2019, pp. 221–38.
63 *Giovanni Bellini. Catalogo illustrato,* 1949, p. 124: "until Dr. Augusto Campana's research on the family who commissioned this painting is known, it is perhaps pointless to revisit this *vexata questio*."
64 G. Ravaioli, "Risorge la Pinacoteca di Rimini," *Giornale dell'Emilia*, March 10, 1949.
65 Rimini, Biblioteca Gambalunga, Carte Campana, box 4, file 4 "Giovanni Bellini," letter from Gino Ravaioli to Augusto Campana, January 19, 1961.
66 Archivio del Museo "Luigi Tonini" in Rimini, fasc. "Giovanni Bellini," letter from Cesare Gnudi to the mayor of Rimini, February 12, 1964.
67 Ibid., estimate attached to the letter of February 12, 1964.
68 Archivio del Museo Luigi Tonini in Rimini, fasc. "Giovanni Bellini", letter from Cesare Gnudi, July 10, 1969.
69 Ibid.
70 P. G. Pasini, "Giovanni Bellini, *Pietà*," in *Sigismondo Pandolfo Malatesta e il suo tempo,* exhibition catalog (Palazzo dell'Arengo, Rimini, 12 July–13 September, 1970), ed. by F. Arduini et al., Vicenza, 1970, pp. 100–01.
71 D. Benati, "Giovanni Bellini, Cristo morto sorretto da quattro angeli," in *Pittura a Rimini tra Gotico e Manierismo,* exhibition catalog (Sala delle Colonne, Rimini, 1 August–30 October, 1979, ed. by C. Volpe and A. Emiliani, Rimini, 1979, pp. 40–43.
72 The exhibitions in which the painting was displayed are: *Uomini denaro istituzioni. L'invenzione del Monte di pietà*, Bologna 2000; *Il potere, le arti, la guerra,* Rimini 2001; *Marco Palmezzano,* Forlì 2005; *Antonello da Messina,* Roma 2006; *Giovanni Bellini,* Roma 2008; *Passion in Venice,* New York 2011; *Gli angeli della Pietà,* Rimini 2012; *Giovanni Bellini dall'icona alla storia,* Milano 2012; *Giovanni Bellini,* Milan 2014; *Piero della Francesca. Indagine su un mito,* Forlì 2016; *Mantegna e Bellini,* London 2018, exhibition that was moved also to Berlin in 2019.
73 Town of Rimini, Executive Decision No. 2031 of August 27, 2018.
74 D. Brullo, "Sgarbi has taken our Bellini to Milan. Very serious," *La Voce di Rimini,* May 27, 2015, p. 13.
75 S.N., "The whole world will be able to see a masterpiece," *La Voce di Rimini,* May 28, 2015, p. 17.
76 Ibid.
77 Zavatta, 2023, pp. 232–33.

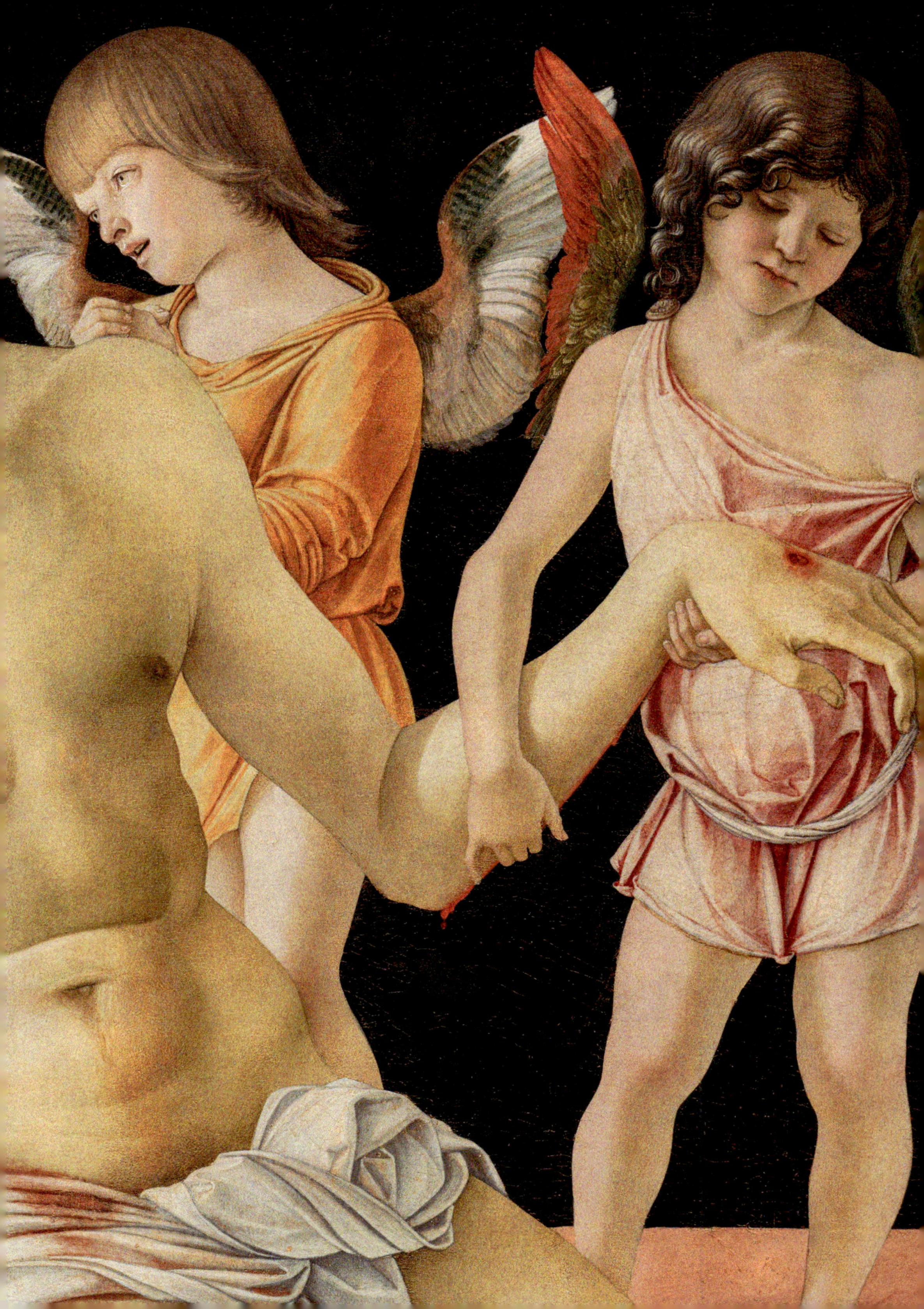

Reconstructing Otello Caprara and Ottorino Nonfarmale's Restoration Work: A Study Based on Oral History and Archival Records

Sara Masinelli

The several conservation and restoration interventions carried out on Giovanni Bellini's *Pietà* (*Dead Christ supported by Four Angels*) constitute a complex and varied narrative, closely tied to the numerous exhibitions in which the work has been displayed, especially during the first half of the twentieth century. Restoration works from 1930 onwards, have been thoroughly documented by Giulio Zavatta, despite the difficulties arising from the absence of any reports in the catalogs of the aforementioned exhibitions.[1]

In 2011, in my M.A. thesis *Il Cristo in Pietà di Giovanni Bellini del Museo della Città di Rimini: vicende storiche e conservative,* I outlined the restoration history of Bellini's *Pietà*, focusing especially on the 1969 restoration by Otello Caprara and Ottorino Nonfarmale, two highly qualified conservators from Bologna.

One of the many obstacles encountered during the drafting of my project was the difficulty in obtaining a detailed report describing the various phases of the intervention. I therefore decided to take an alternative approach: I combined oral history—provided directly by conservators, their heirs and professionals, who, in more recent times, had been involved in the day-to-day maintenance of the painting—with archival documents and photographs. This method, largely based on recollections, naturally involves significant risks and uncertainties. Far from claiming to deliver absolute truth or an account precise in every detail, the essay seeks to provide insights and observations to support further study and investigation.

The ongoing restoration project carried out by CBC – Conservazione Beni Culturali—promoted by Venetian Heritage—together with the need for a better understanding of past interventions, provides the first significant opportunity to publicly share the results of my research.

Condition assessment and conservation attempt on the wooden panel

On November 21, 1968, the Soprintendenza alle Gallerie of Bologna sends the following communication to the Italian Ministry of Public Education (Antiquities and Fine Arts Department):

> This Office has for some time been considering the condition of the painting depicting the *Dead Christ and two angels* by Giovanni Bellini, kept in the Pinacoteca Civica of Rimini. Unfortunately, the examination of the panel, which is completely corroded and lacking any consistency, has convinced this Soprintendenza of the need for a transfer. The exceptional importance of the work has prompted this Office to seek a higher opinion before proceeding with the urgent restoration work.[2]

On February 28, 1969, the Director of the Cultural Institutes of the Town of Rimini, informs the Soprintendenza that the painting has been delivered to conservators Otello Caprara and Ottorino Nonfarmale, recommending "the utmost swiftness in the restoration work," to make it possible for the painting to be returned and displayed in the pinacoteca by the following summer season.[3]

From the very first analysis of the painting, it becomes clear that the panel has already undergone several restorations and that the integrity of the whole artwork has been seriously compromised by the critical condition of the wooden support. Upon examination of the wooden boards, it emerges that these have been cut tangentially, an unsuitable technique for preventing warping and the wood has been used despite presenting numerous knots. The back of the painting features a so-called 'Florentine' cradling

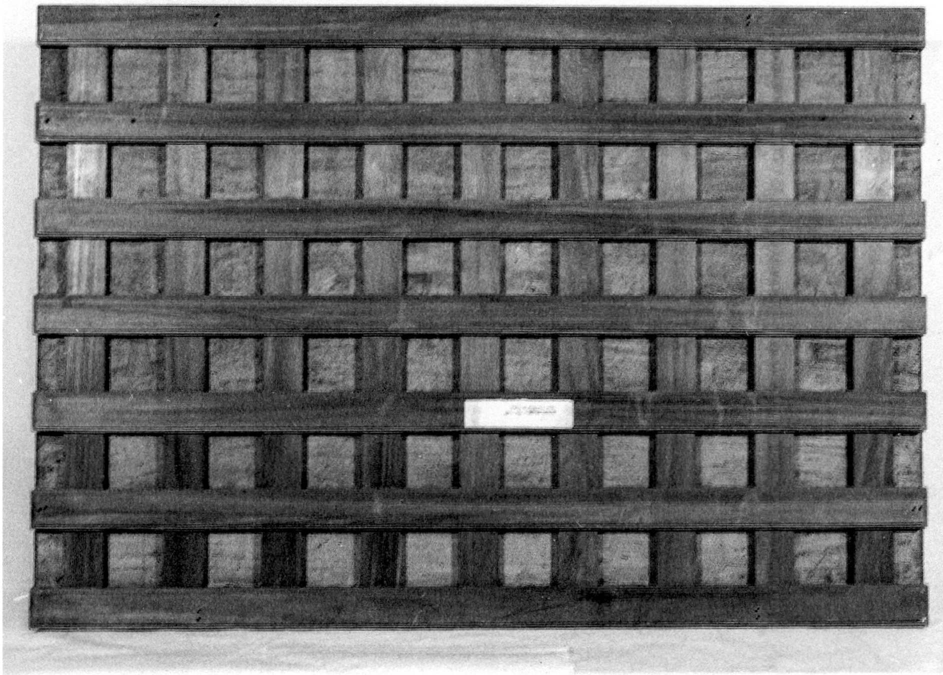

1
The painting before the 1969 restoration work seen from the back, with the 'Florentine' cradling system

system, a wooden latticework that has accelerated the deterioration of the material underneath (fig. 1). Furthermore, the sliding crossbars of the rigid restraint have now lost their function and appear to be stuck.[4] The painting has also been negatively affected by the thinning of the panel, a procedure to which it was subjected when the cradling was applied. To further complicate the situation, the wooden panel shows widespread damage from wood-boring insects and the sapwood appears to be severely riddled with holes. All these issues combine to undermine the stability of the paint layers. Therefore, the decision is taken by the conservators to remove the wooden latticework immediately. Careful observation of the photographic documentation suggests that Caprara proceeds gradually, working on the panel little by little as the cradling system is removed. The conservators also remove the wooden dowels used to join the boards, replacing them with higher-quality ones consisting of triangular wooden inserts.

As stated in a report from Cesare Gnudi dated July 1969,[5] despite all the efforts to consolidate the wooden support of the painting, the deterioration process cannot be reversed. Once the Ministry's authorization is obtained, the decision is therefore taken to transfer the painted surface from the old panel to a new canvas, and the painting is promptly moved to Nonfarmale's restoration workshop for repair.[6]

Ottorino Nonfarmale's testimony: the transfer of the painted surface

The continuous requests for assessments, verification, photos and tests to which the panel has been subjected, testify to the caution with which this delicate procedure was undertaken. During our interview,[7] Ottorino Nonfarmale explained in detail the various stages of the intervention. First, the overpainting was removed and the peeling paint was consolidated, where possible, using 30% diluted Paraloid B72. The conservator informed us that Japanese paper, cut into squares of approximately 10-12 cm per side[8], was applied twice to the painted surface (fig. 2). Once the paper had completely dried out, and following the application of a cotton canvas, Paraloid was applied again to the entire surface. After a further drying period of ten to fifteen days, a hemp canvas, washed three times in boiling water and ironed to perfection, was also applied. The goal was to create a lining on the painted surface that would protect it during the delicate stages of the intervention. The removal of the wooden panel was conducted manually, working from the back with gouges and chisels, along with tweezers in the areas that required greater precision (fig. 3). Once the original panel was removed, the gesso ground layer was lightly cleaned and minor conservation work was carried out on four or five areas that showed signs of fragility. The fact that two coats of gesso ground were originally

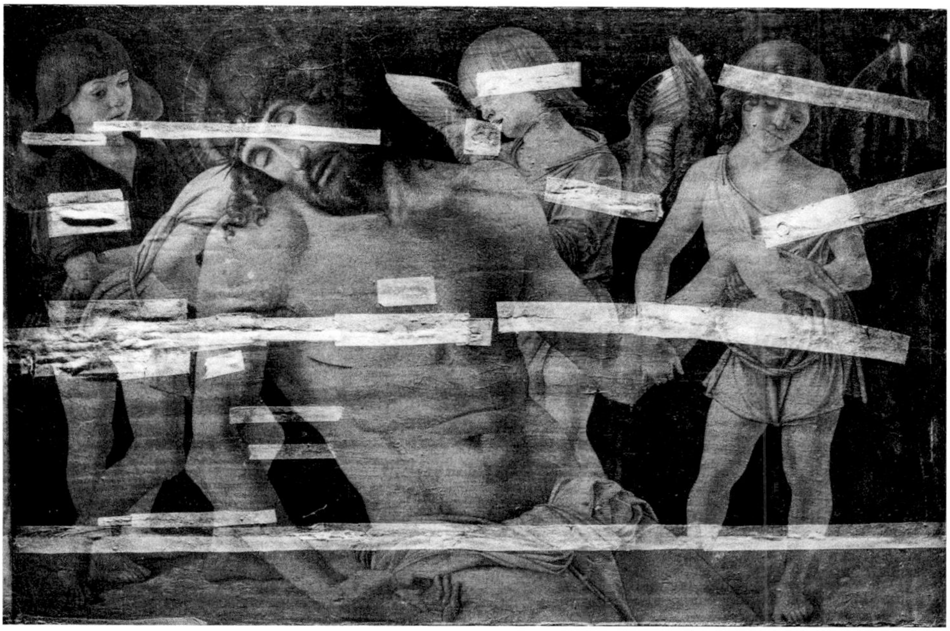

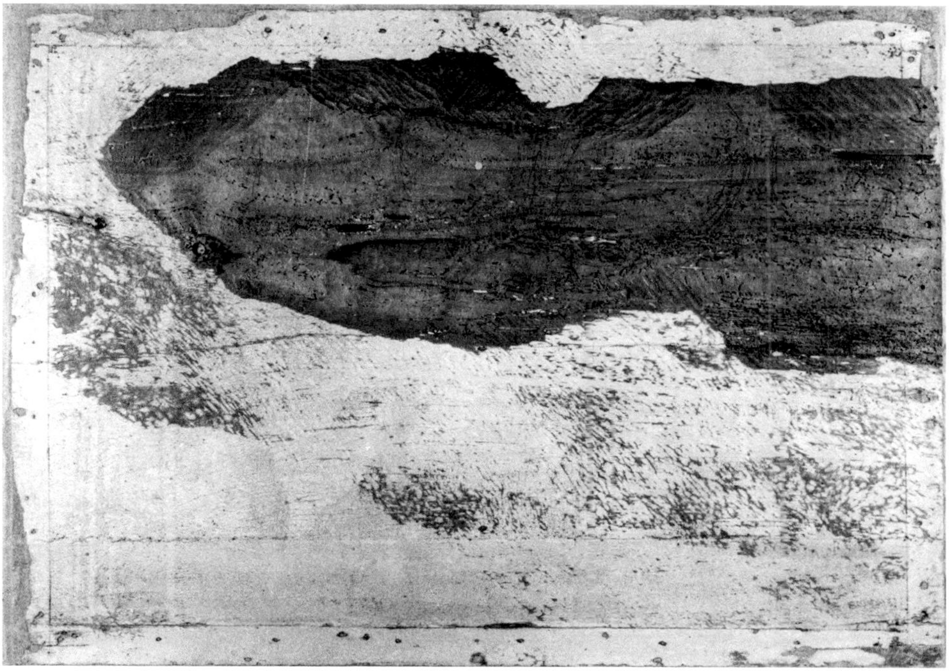

2
1969 restoration work: fixing the painted surface with Japanese paper

3
1969 restoration work: mechanical removal of the wooden support

applied—as prescribed by the most authoritative ancient treatises on painting—contributed to the stability of the painted surface.

The back of the painting was consolidated with three coats of highly diluted dewaxed shellac, onto which the first layer of cotton canvas was glued, using a casein softened with animal glue and Bologna chalk. A further coat of shellac was then applied to isolate the mestica from moisture and a final layer of hemp canvas was then added.

Once all the layers had catalyzed, the painting was laid out on a flat surface and the protective lining was gradually and completed removed using solvent, ensuring constant blotting to eliminate any excess adhesive: first the hemp canvas, then the two layers of cotton gauze, and finally the layer of Japanese paper. On the reverse, a 2mm thick sheet of expanded polystyrene was applied to ensure the reversibility of the intervention, to prevent condensation and to facilitate any future separation of the painting from the new support, consisting of an anodized aluminum frame and resin-embedded mesh.

Finally, in addition to some necessary fillings, watercolor retouching was carried out and completed with the application of a thin layer of Winsor & Newton matte varnish. Despite some doubts raised in the 1970s,[9] the restoration is now almost unanimously regarded as a breakthrough intervention, conducted with the utmost skill and care: a transfer that ensures reversibility and, despite the loss of the original wooden support, fully preserves the aesthetic quality and characteristics of the original work.

1 G. Zavatta, "Giovanni Bellini's Pietà di Rimini: exhibitions and restorations (1930–2019)," *Storia dell'arte*, no. 2, July–December 2022, pp. 27–47

2 Archivio della Soprintendenza alle Gallerie per le province di Bologna, Ferrara, Forlì e Ravenna, FO 63, prot. no. 1490 of 11/21/1968 (Musei Nazionali di Bologna - Direzione regionale Musei Nazionali Emilia Romagna).

3 Rimini, Biblioteca Gambalunga, Archivio Biblioteca, pos. IX, ref. no. 165 of 28/02/1969.

4 The 'Florentine' cradling system was applied by Mauro Pellicioli in 1930. For more information on Pellicioli's restoration work, see Giulio Zavatta's essay in the present volume.

5 Archivio Museo Luigi Tonini di Rimini, file 'Giovanni Bellini', letter from Cesare Gnudi, July 10, 1969. See also Giulio Zavatta's essay in the present volume.

6 Archivio della Soprintendenza alle Gallerie per le province di Bologna, Ferrara, Forlì e Ravenna, FO 63, prot. no. 8179 of 06/18/1969 (Musei Nazionali di Bologna - Direzione regionale Musei Nazionali Emilia Romagna).

7 The meeting with Ottorino Nonformale took place at his restoration workshop in San Lazzaro di Savena in the fall of 2010. Nonfarmale described both the attempt to save the wooden support and the transferring of the painted surface to canvas.

8 It is likely that the first phase of this operation was carried out before the painting was moved to the restoration workshop, in order to minimize any risk of damage to the painted surface.

9 Archivio della Soprintendenza alle Gallerie per le province di Bologna, Ferrara, Forlì e Ravenna, FO 113, prot. no. 2925 of 12/21/1973 (Musei Nazionali di Bologna - Direzione regionale Musei Nazionali Emilia Romagna). The then Soprintendente Cesare Gnudi wrote the following to the mayor of Rimini, Nicola Pagliarani: "I have received several reports from various sources about publicly expressed and not entirely informed judgments on the restoration of Giovanni Bellini's *Ecce Homo*; a restoration, as you well remember, carried out at the expense of the State by this Office, performed by restorers of the highest international standing and under the supervision of the Higher Council of Antiquities and Fine Arts. It is therefore difficult to accept that, in contexts lacking in technical or scientific expertise, such exaggerated and exclusively polemical judgments are being made."

Technical Insights

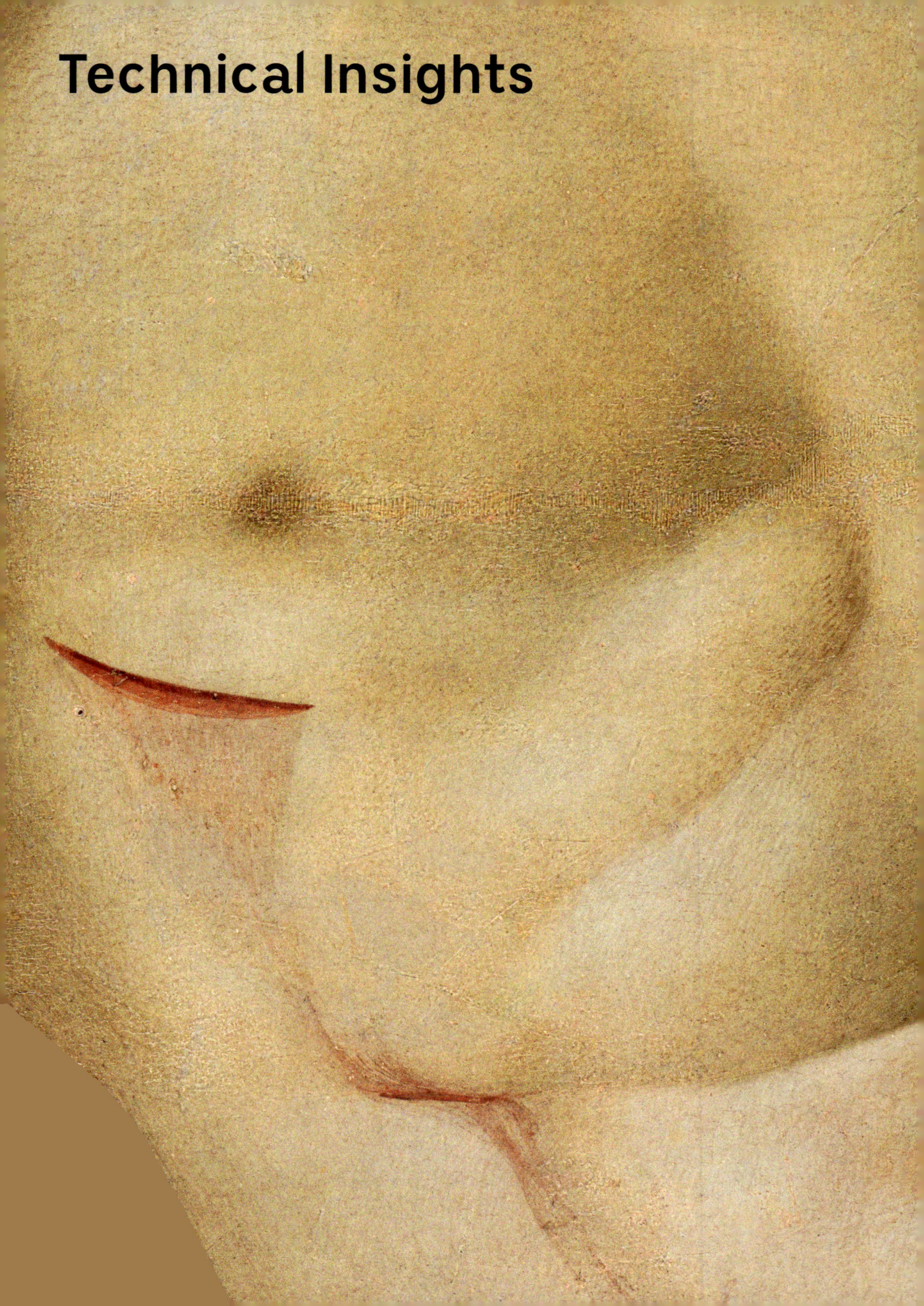

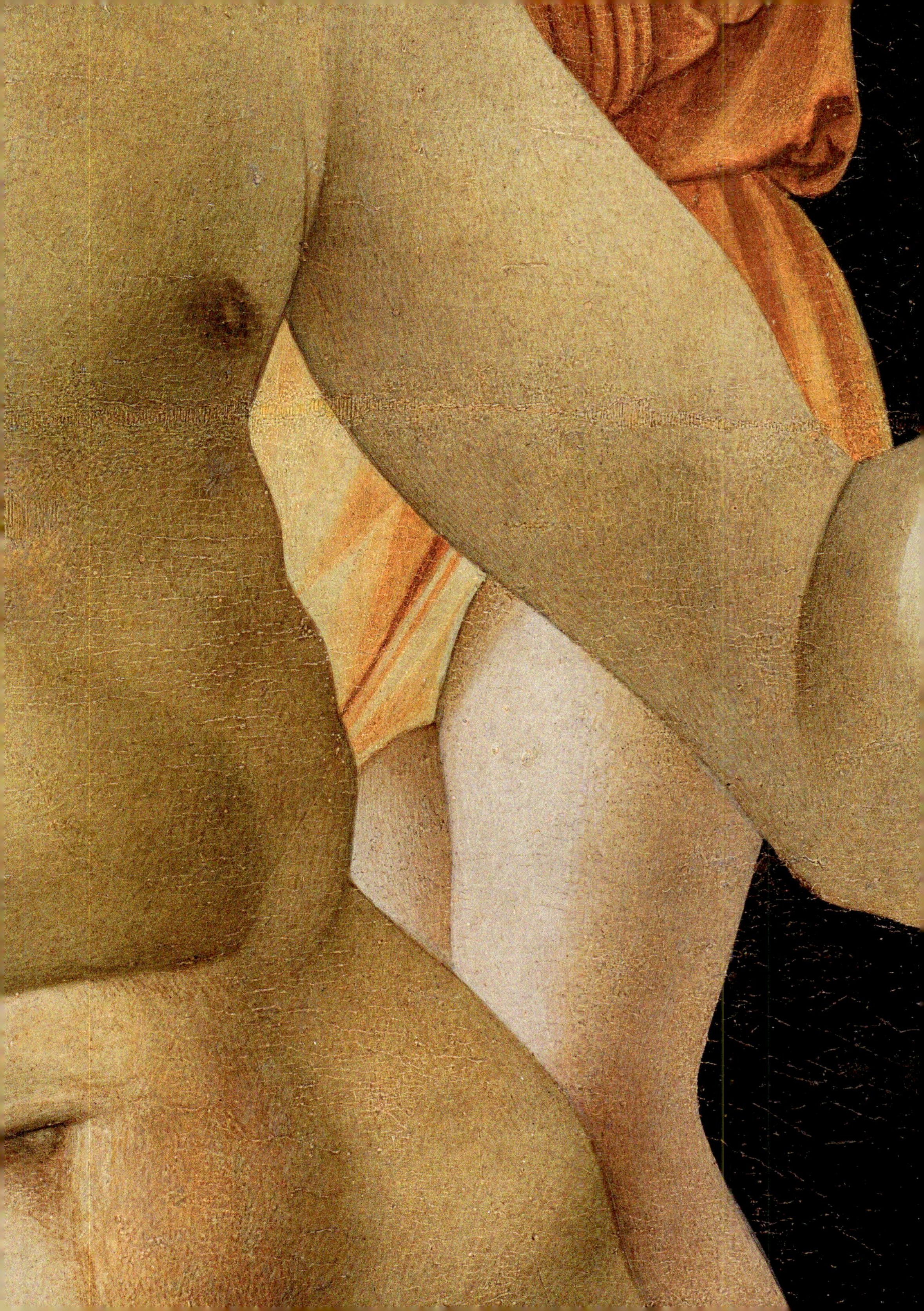

Diagnostic Exams for the Pre-Restoration Study of Giovanni Bellini's *Pietà*

Maria Francesca Alberghina and Salvatore Schiavone

During the study and planning phase of the restoration of the painting *Pietà* (*Dead Christ supported by Four Angels*) kept in the Museo della Città di Rimini "Luigi Tonini", a series of non-invasive diagnostic exams were carried out, including UV fluorescence, direct digital X-ray, IR reflectography using a 1700 nm InGaAs scanner, False Color IR, and X-ray fluorescence (XRF) spectroscopy. The primary goal was to document the condition of the work and provide a preliminary identification of the pigments to support the upcoming conservation intervention. A second goal was to gather evidence of the painting's peculiarities and the techniques employed, for future comparison with the results of studies of Bellini's other works,[1] to better understand the chronological development of his *modus pingendi.*

Using UV LEDs (365 nm) to induce fluorescence, the distribution and condition of the thick aged layer of protective varnish was documented, the fillings were differentiated, and the few areas of repainting over the varnish were identified, as well as the micro-gaps in the underpainting and the areas showing anomalies such as browning, detachments, and fracture lines in the thin paint film. The IRFC image provided an initial map of the chromophores, thanks to their characteristic spectral response (fig. 1), which were subsequently identified using XRF. Chemical examinations on areas without retouching or additions evidenced the use of a palette consistent with that reported in the literature on Bellini. In particular,

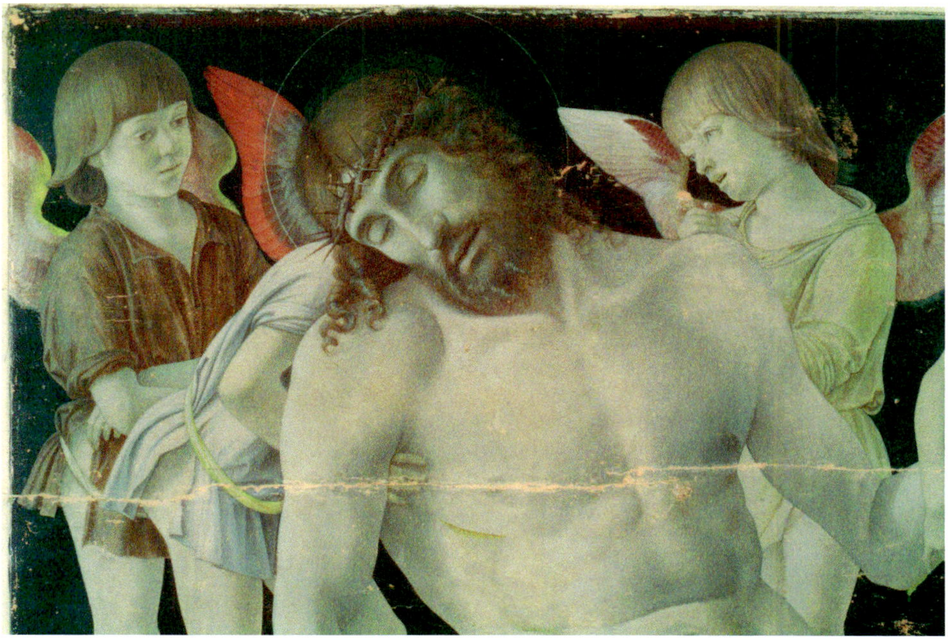

1
Giovanni Bellini, *Pietà*, False Color Infrared image of the painting, detail, Rimini, Museo della Città "Luigi Tonini"

the following materials were verified for use: lead white, lead and tin yellow, red lacquer, vermilion/cinnabar, a copper-based green pigment, and pigments based on iron oxides and clay minerals (ochre or earth). In the case of the vivid blue layers on the angels' wings, the examination suggests the use of lapis lazuli or indigo mixed or superimposed with small amounts of azurite.

The paint layers are characterized by low radiodensity, due to their thinness and the type of mixtures, making them difficult to read in the radiographic image. The predominant response is, in fact, that of the support structure, consisting of a grid of hollow aluminum and a perforated fiberglass sheet onto which the painting was glued after being transferred from panel to canvas—an operation not detectable in X-ray.

The grid is anchored to the frame of the painting by plates and screws, while the canvas is attached to the frame by nails. The fiberglass sheet is not visible from the back as a thick layer of filler conceals it. High contrast reflectography (fig. 2) has revealed the lines of the underdrawing, executed in

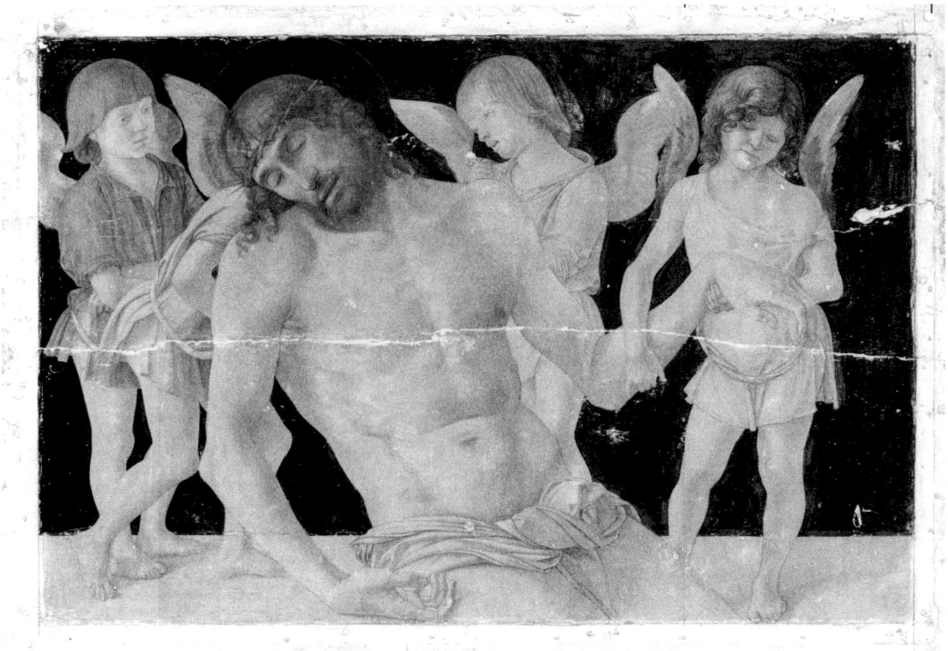

2
Giovanni Bellini, *Pietà*,
IR reflectography acquired using
a 1700 nm Ingas scanner, Rimini,
Museo della Città "Luigi Tonini"

black pigment applied freehand with a brush. The lines are visible along the drapery and both the outer and inner contours of the figures. The drawing varies in direction and thickness, reflecting the artist's intention either to incorporate the black line into the final chromatic definition or, in the more diluted or finer strokes, to conceal it entirely beneath the final paint layers. Parallel oblique lines of varying density are also visible, used to define the shadows.[2] The area of the wing of the angel bending behind Christ is also clearly visible in the image: the dark blue layer, whose perimeter is difficult to distinguish from the black background when viewed normally, is clearly visible with reflectogram due to the different response of the blue pigment and the other pigments present in the underlying layer. Neither the X-radiograph nor the reflectography revealed any *pentimenti* or changes in the composition; the 1700 nm IR image shows only a slight adjustment of the pink robe of one of the angels on the right side of the composition. One can discern the preparation of the figures, which were outlined from the start without any overlapping by the underpaintings. The X-ray, IR, and UV fluorescence images all confirm the stability of the current support. In the case of the paint film and the underlying layers, anomalies or degradation are observed, associated with thinning caused by the loss of layers over time or past cleaning of the work. Finally, the crack in the painting surface, generated by the movements of the original wooden support and running longitudinally across the entire width of the painting, is well documented in terms of its extent and the pattern of the margins.

1 A. Braham, M. Wyld, J. Plesters, "Bellini's 'The Blood of the Redeemer'," vol. 2, pp. 11–24; G. Poldi and G. C. F. Villa, "A New Examination of Giovanni Bellini's 'Pesaro Altarpiece': Recent Findings and Comparisons with Other Works by Bellini," in *Studying Old Master Paintings: Technology and Practice. The National Gallery Technical Bulletin 30th Anniversary Conference*, Conference preceedings (London, 16–18 September 2009), ed. by M. Spring, London, 2011, pp. 28–36; L. de Viguerie *et al.*, "An Investigation of Bellini's *Transfiguration* in the Capodimonte Museum by Means of XRF and Visible Reflectance Hyperspectral Imaging: Bellini's Handling of Materials in the Head and Figure of the Transfigured Christ, *Heritage Science*, vol. 11, no. 163, 2023: https://doi.org/10.1186/s40494-023-01001-7.

2 The results of the examination fit well with G. Villa's discussion of the development of Bellini's preparatory drawing: "It was between the late 1460s and the mid-1480s that Bellini drew, over the primer and the possible imprimatura, a very light drawing with a very neat, short, diagonal hatching, which plays with the intensity by overlapping or not the brushstroke, within outlines defined by a dark, segmented brushstroke, executed with a thicker brush, sometimes cut short so as to gradually recalibrate the intensity of the shapes. A flexible monochrome hatching for a schematic partitioning of the light planes. As he matured, Bellini thinned this contour line, thickening the graphic lines, executed with an increasingly fine brush beneath a now glazed and translucent pictorial material. In the 1890s, the outline of the images became cursive, no longer structured in individual brushstrokes linked to one another, as the hand moves freely over the primer as long as the brush is supported by the ink; at the same time, the chiaroscuro and modular hatching becomes lighter and then disappears, when, towards the end of the century, using first the brush and then the charcoal, only the main lines of the composition and figurative groups were drawn, leaving it to the now fully mastered color to give life to the forms.": G. C. F. Villa, "Indagando Bellini. Quattro ancone in un itinerario," in G. Poldi, G. C. F. Villa, *Indagando Bellini*, Milan, 2009, pp. 13–160, esp. pp. 14–15

The Restoration of the Artwork

Lucia Tito

The restoration work on Giovanni Bellini's *Pietà* (*Dead Christ supported by Four Angels*), kept in the Museo della Città di Rimini "Luigi Tonini" was limited to the painted surface (fig. 1). The aluminum lattice support structure and its anchoring system were thoroughly examined, and the results of the tests were entirely satisfactory, ruling out the need for any structural intervention. Results confirm that the transfer of the painting, carried out in 1969 by Otello Caprara and Ottorino Nonfarmale, while undoubtedly a very invasive and risky operation, was performed in an exemplary manner (fig. 2).

Thanks to the photographic documentation in the Archivio Fotografico Ministeriale di Bologna, it has been possible to partially reconstruct the characteristics of the removed panel. We know it measured 91 × 130.5 cm, although the thickness is unknown. It probably consisted of two poplar boards arranged longitudinally, the bottom one being only 18 cm high. The crack that runs horizontally across the upper part of the painting does not, therefore, coincide with the joint between the two boards, as one might mistakenly assume, but is the result of the movements in the panel caused by heat and humidity variations, which most likely caused a crack in the larger upper board (fig. 3). The restoration by Mauro Pellicioli in the 1930s, with the application of a 'Florentine' cradling on the back, actually aggravated the condition of the panel, and ultimately made it necessary to transfer the painted surface.

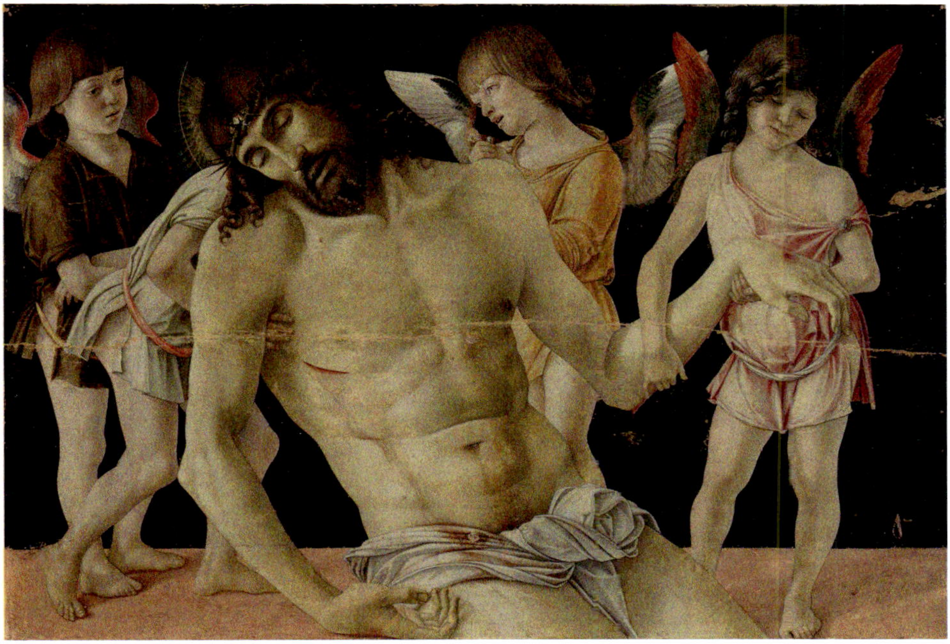

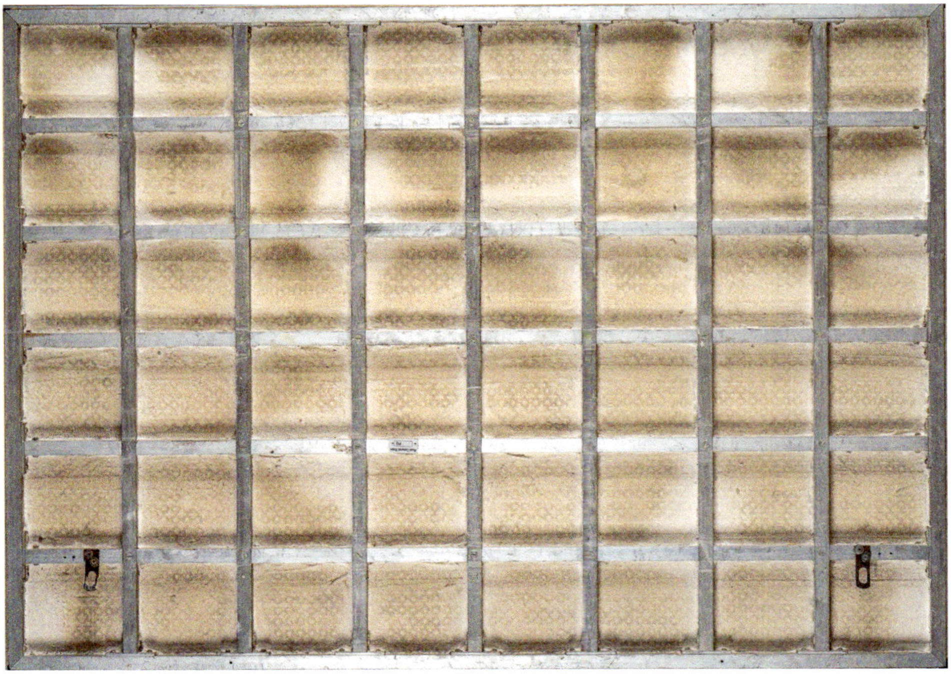

1
Giovanni Bellini, *Pietà*, the painting before the latest restoration, Rimini, Museo della Città "Luigi Tonini"

2
Giovanni Bellini, *Pietà*, back of the painting with a lattice aluminum support structure, made in 1969, Rimini, Museo della Città "Luigi Tonini"

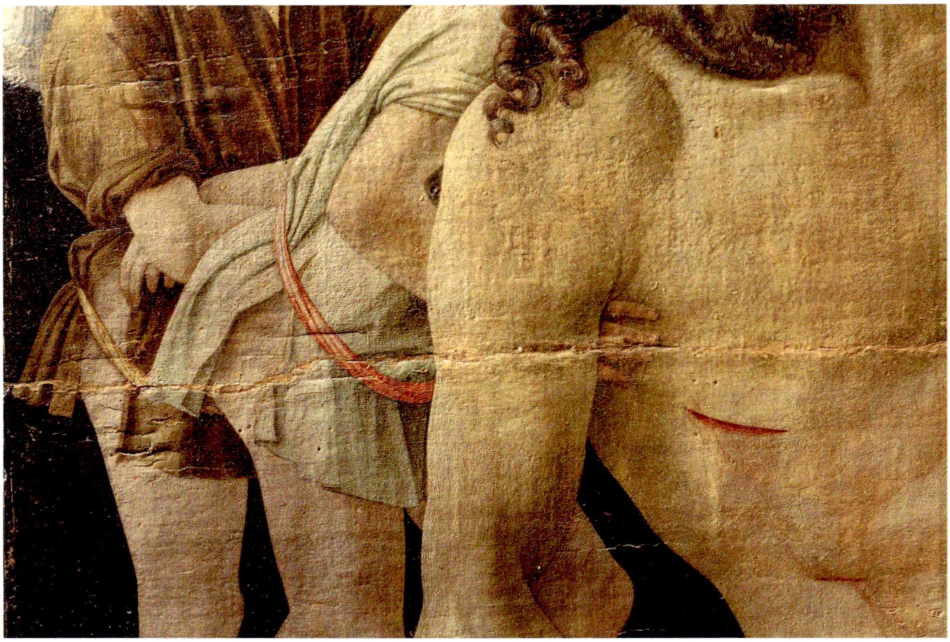

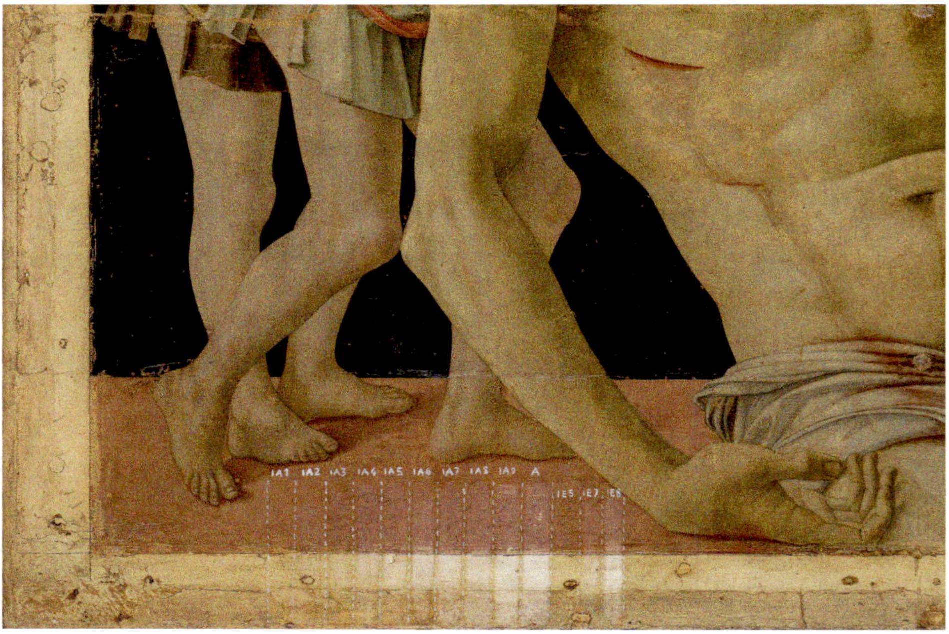

3
Giovanni Bellini, *Pietà*, detail of the painting photographed under raking light, Rimini, Museo della Città "Luigi Tonini"

4
Giovanni Bellini, *Pietà*, Solubility test, Rimini, Museo della Città "Luigi Tonini"

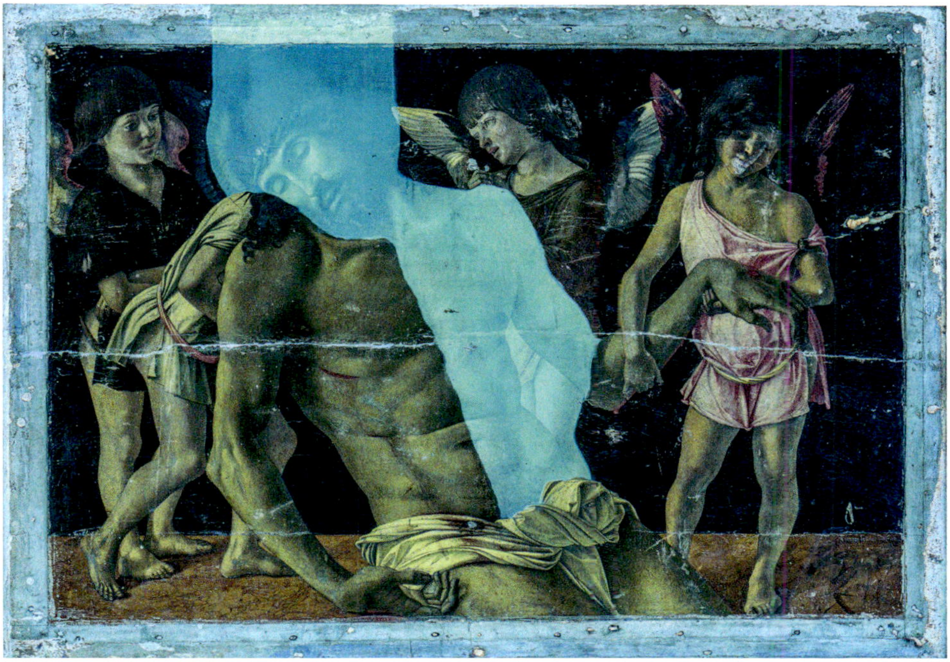

5
Giovanni Bellini, *Pietà*, cleaning test area under UV reflected light, Rimini, Museo della Città "Luigi Tonini"

As already suggested, the main problems identified during the present restoration concerned the painted surface. Issues included drip marks and abrasions on the paint film left by an old, very invasive cleaning, and the presence of a heavily yellowed varnish—probably pigmented—applied during the last intervention to even out the surface and mask color losses, the varnish having altered to the point of compromising the appearance of the original colors. After conducting accurate solubility tests (fig. 4), the altered varnish layer was removed using a three-part mixture of solvents (isooctane, 45%; acetone, 40%; and alcohol, 15%), thereby revealing the original paint film without affecting its surface in any way (fig. 5).

The central crack, as well as the woodworm holes and deeper abrasions, were filled with a mixture of Bologna chalk and rabbit-skin glue, then retouched with watercolor and Gamblin varnish, using hatching to restore visual continuity to the colors while leaving the intervention discernible. Minor abrasions were harmonized with the adjacent areas using glazes.

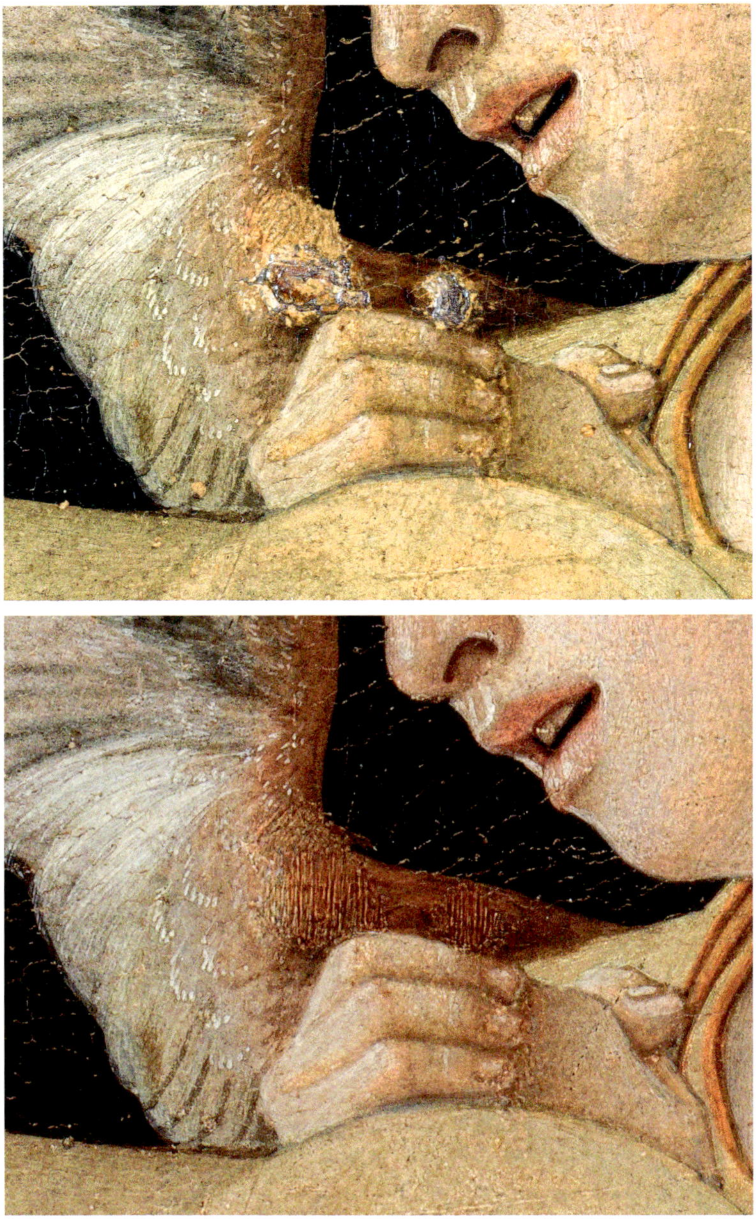

6
Giovanni Bellini, *Pietà*, detail of the putto with joined hands, before and after restoration, Rimini, Museo della Città "Luigi Tonini"

7
Giovanni Bellini, *Pietà*, the painting after the removal of the heavily yellowed varnish, Rimini, Museo della Città "Luigi Tonini"

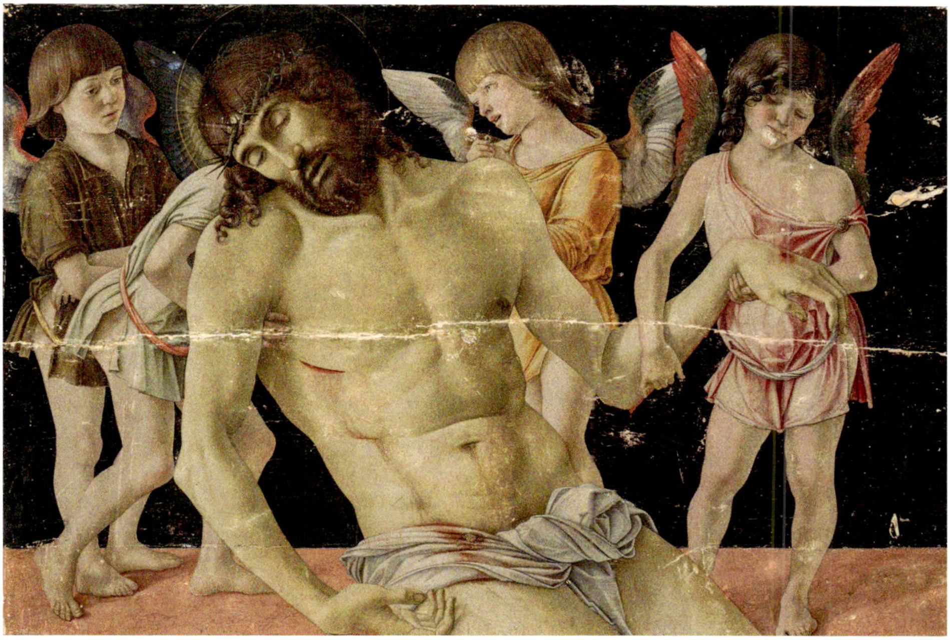

The holes left by the nails of the original crossbars were filled and restored using both hatching and tone reduction, in line with the project supervisors' suggestions from the Italian Ministry of Culture. The intervention on the hand of the angel behind Christ's right shoulder was particularly significant, making it possible to restore the original aspect of the putto clasped hands, and showing that they were not intended, as hypothesized in the past, to be holding a nail symbolizing the Passion (fig. 6). Some apparently discordant elements, such as the brownish hue on Christ's abdomen, were toned down but not eliminated, being evidence of Bellini's pictorial method and, in particular, of the stratigraphic succession of the different painting layers.

At the end of the process (fig. 7), a Retoucher Lefranc & Bourgeois varnish with UV filter was first applied by brush and then sprayed. The entire intervention was extensively documented with photos, using macro photographs to evidence the differences in the preparatory layer of the painting, particularly visible on the edges. Nowhere in the work were signs found of a warm-tone preparation. In all areas where it was visible (scratches, abrasions, etc), the imprimatura appeared white and, upon further investigation, consisted of white lead.

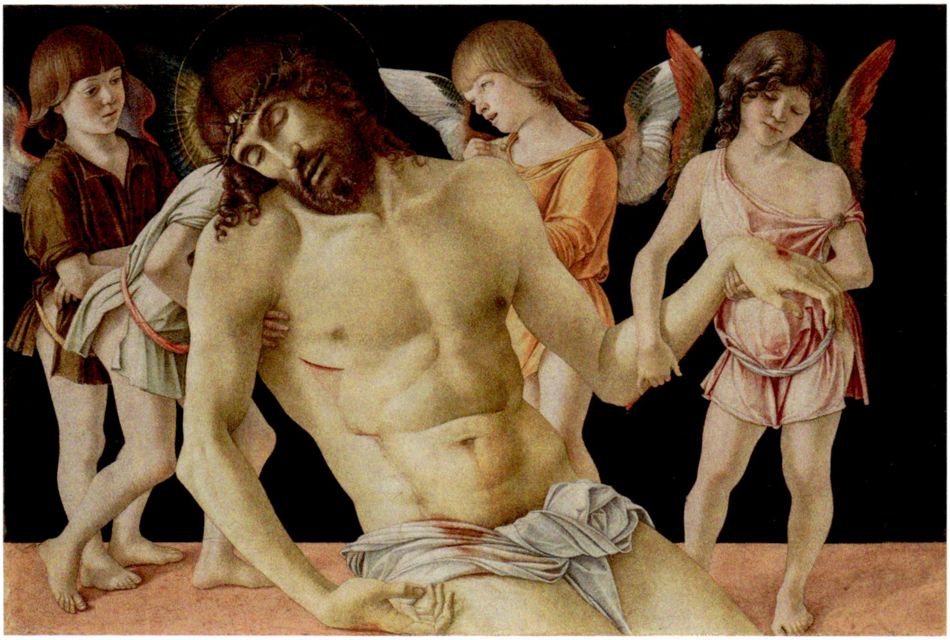

8
Giovanni Bellini, *Pietà*, the painting after restoration by Lucia Tito, Rimini, Museo della Città "Luigi Tonini"

Overall, the restoration can be described as a delicate and respectful maintenance and aesthetic revision, aimed at restoring the legibility and chromatic balance of the work and reducing the effects of alterations, without erasing the traces of the painting's complex conservation history. All this for the purpose of making it possible to better appreciate the original intentions of the great Venetian master (fig. 8).

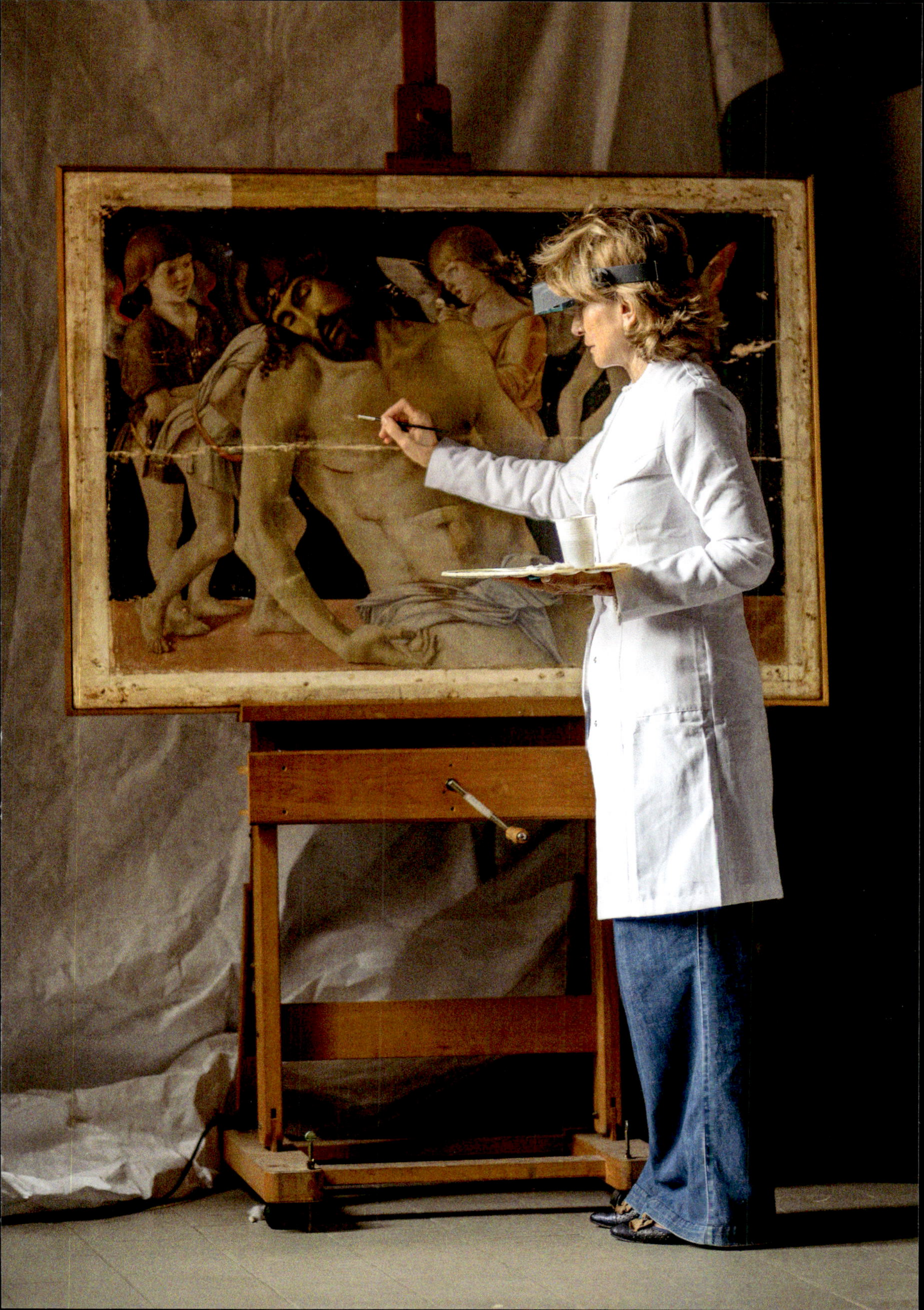

Fondazione Venetian Heritage, Venice

Venetian Heritage Inc., New York

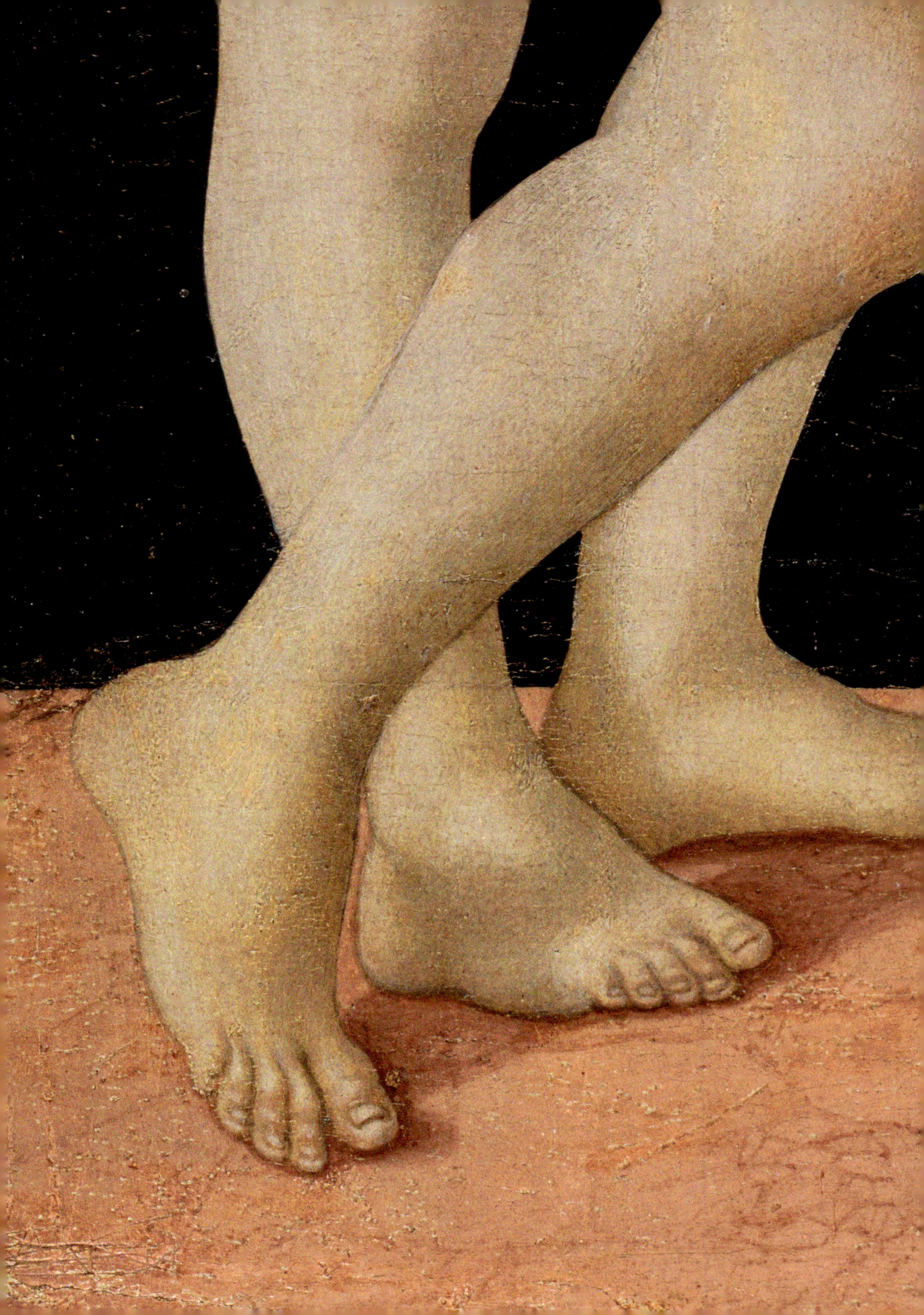

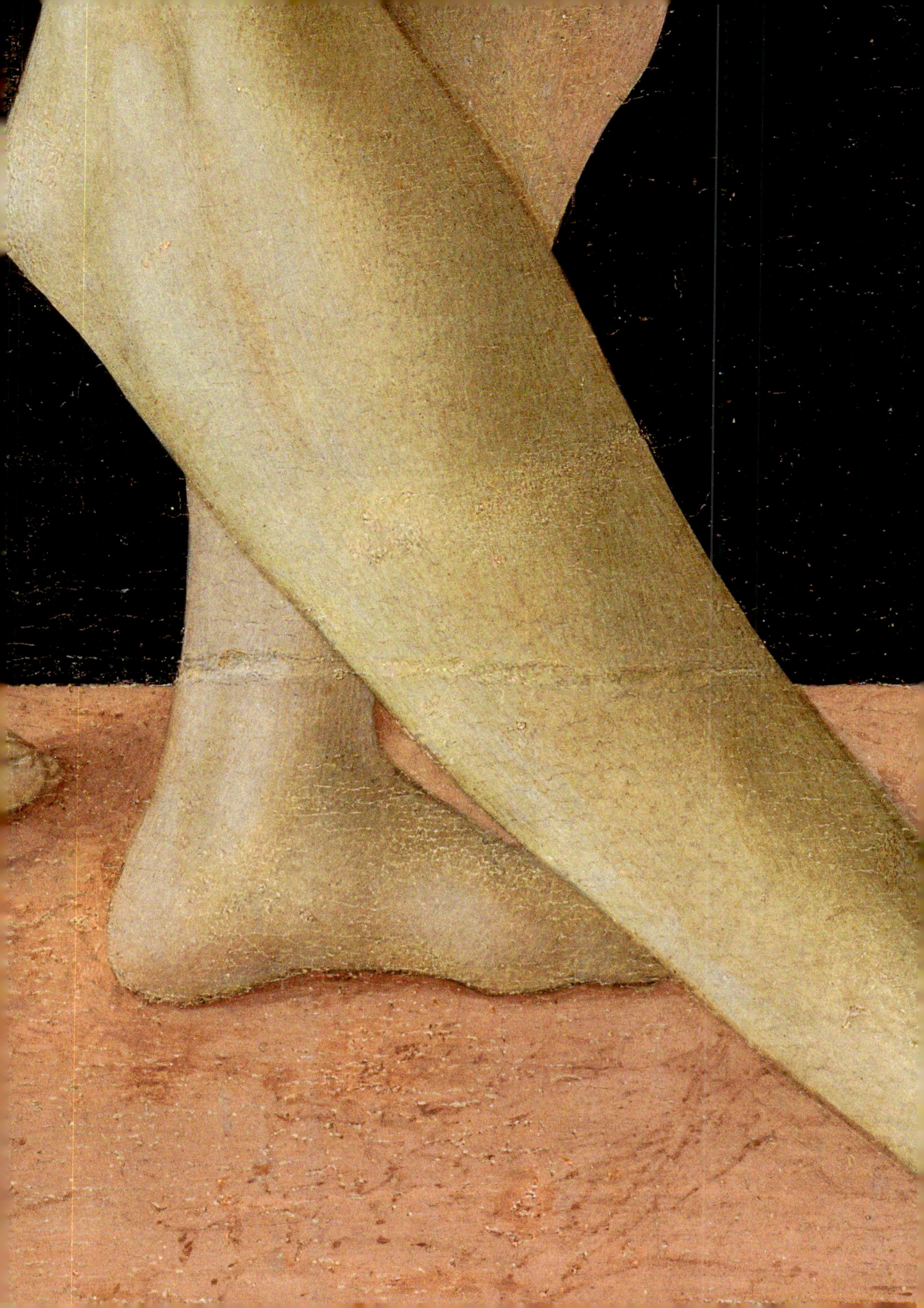

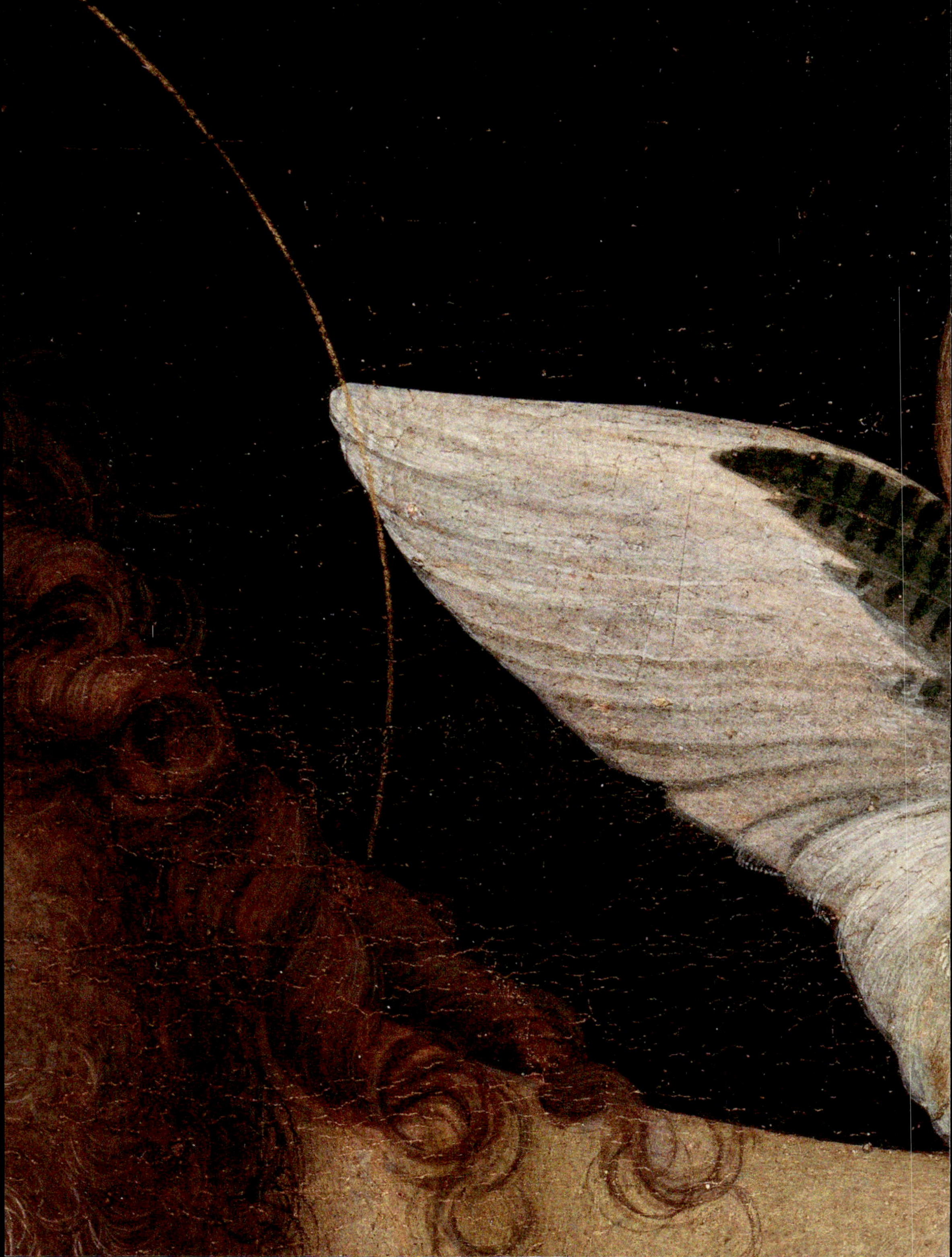

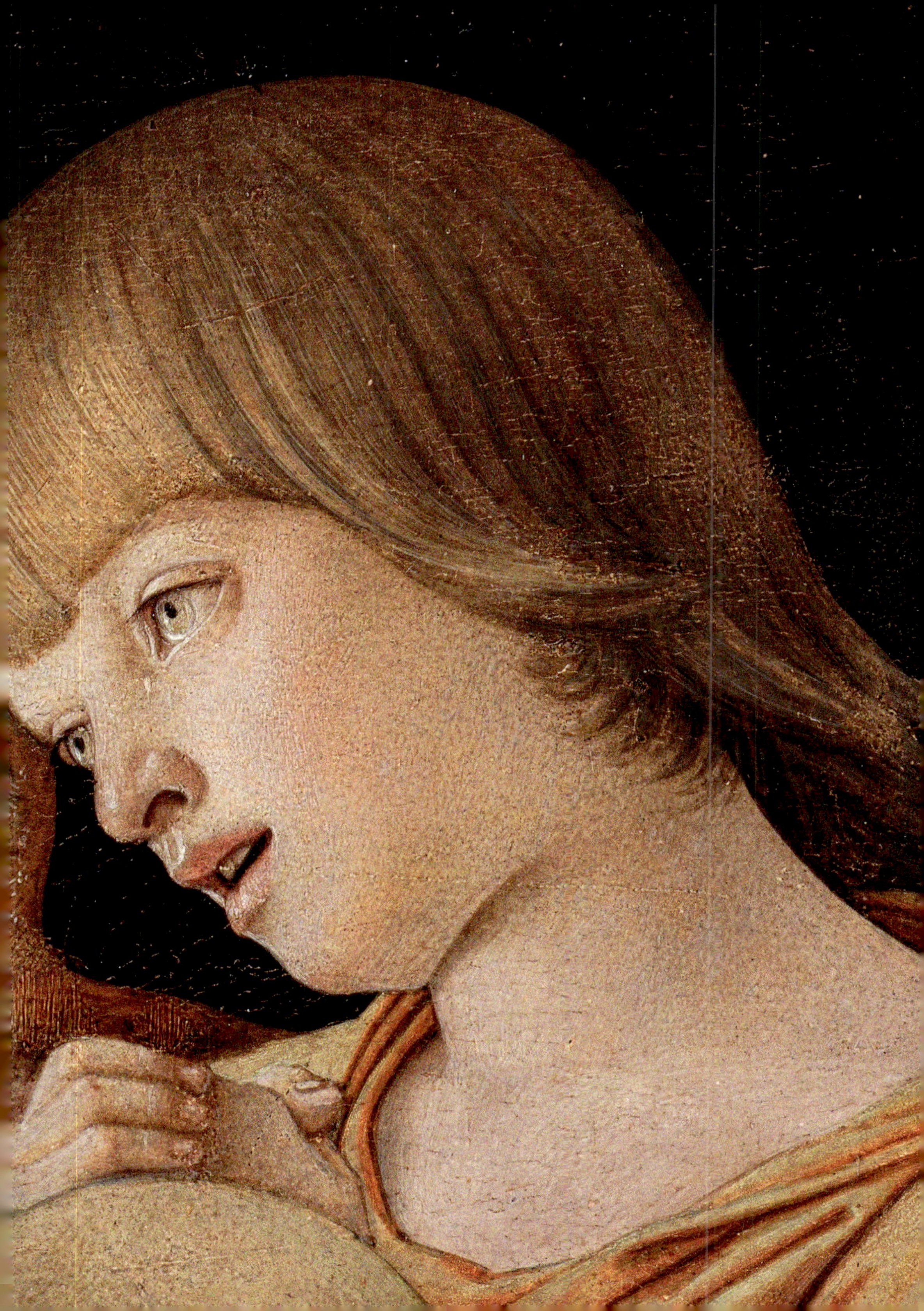

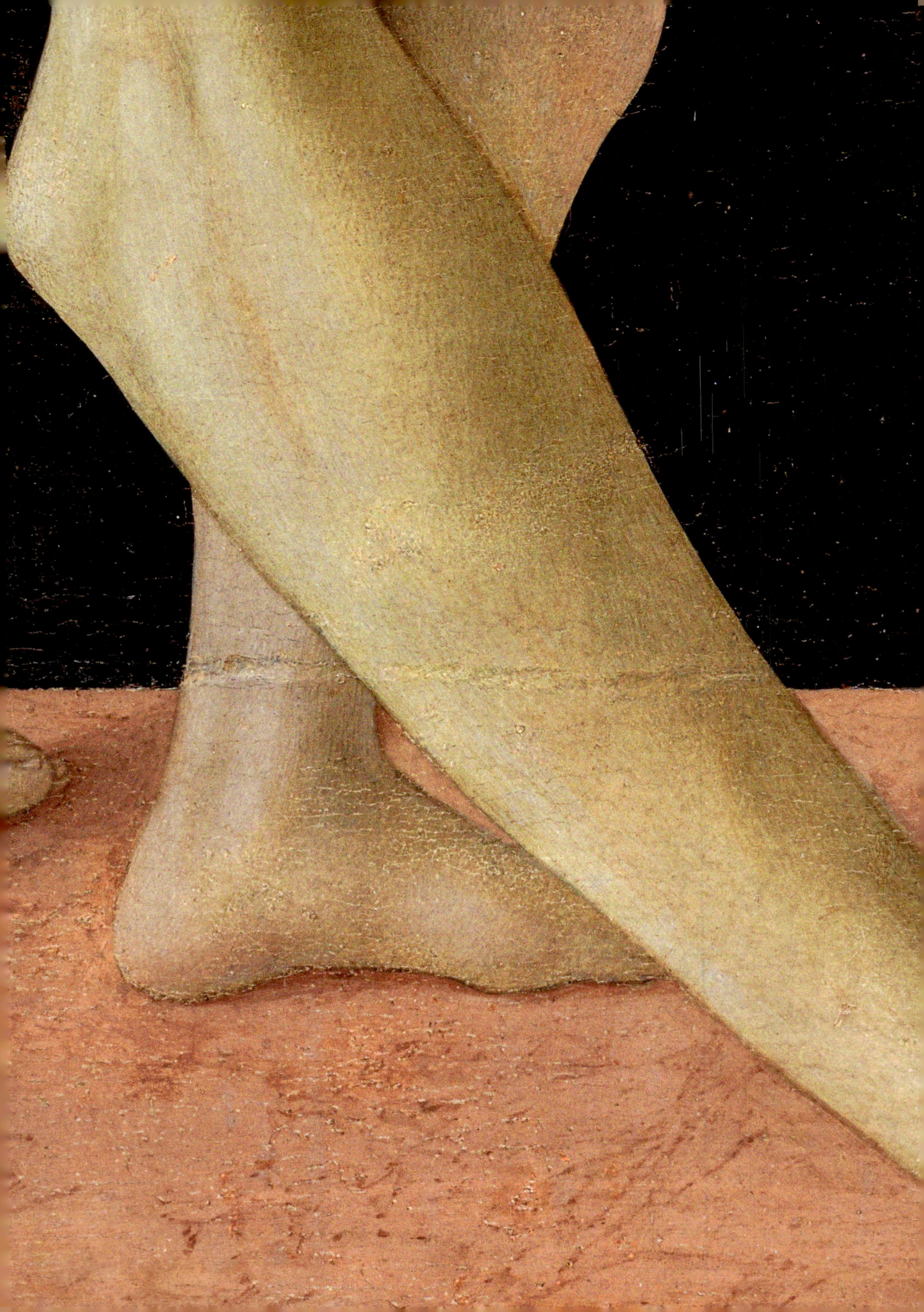

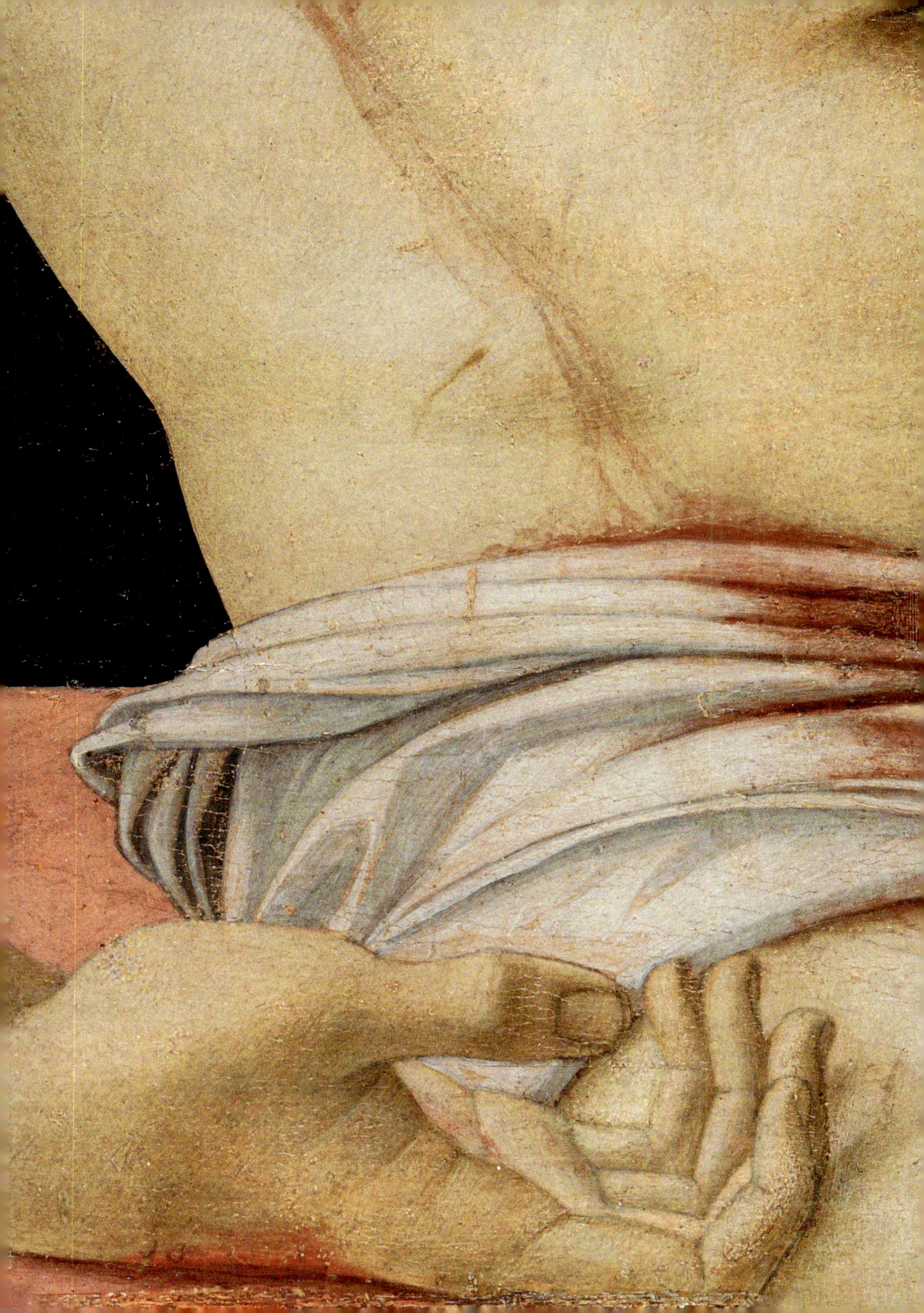

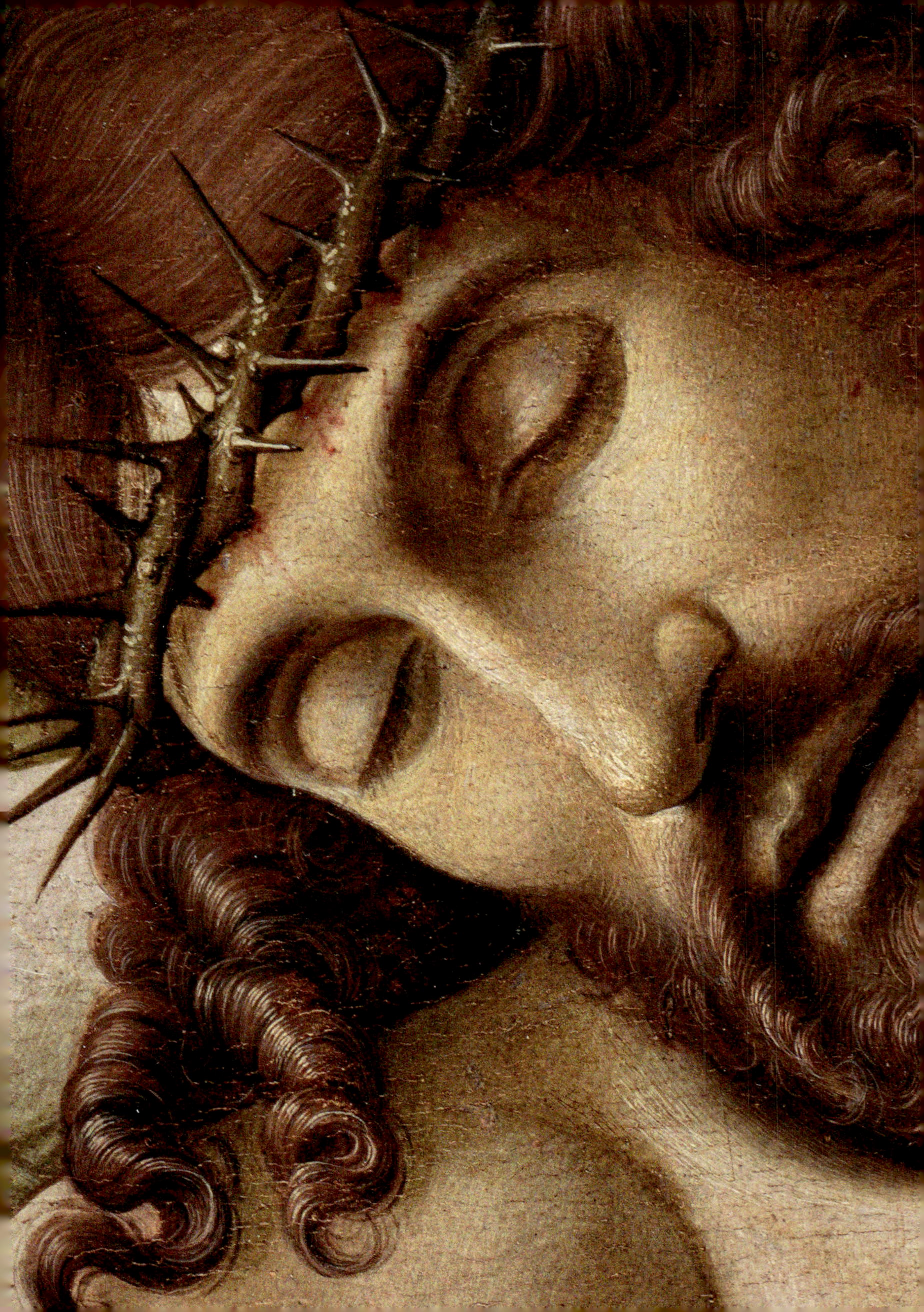